Elaborate Cooking Uncovered

By

Ali Javaheri

BARNY BOOKS

First published in Great Britain in 2005 by Barny Books
All rights reserved

ISBN No: 1 903172 36 5

Published by:

        Barny Books
        Hough on the Hill
        Near Grantham
        Lincolnshire
        NG32 2BB

        Tel: 01400 250246

Printed by:

        Athenaeum Press Ltd
        Dukesway
        Team Valley
        Gateshead
        Tyne & Wear
        NE11 0PZ

        Tel: 0191 4910770

Dedication

For

Sayeh and Simon

whom I love so very much

and my mother

for giving me the inspiration and

encouragement

CONTENTS

Contents Continued

Introduction

During the 30 years I have lived in England, I have watched with pleasure the curiosity and interest my friends and customers have shown as they have enjoyed my exotic and delicate dishes from around the world. It was their urging that prompted me to commit my knowledge of international cuisine experience to paper.

This book goes right back to basics and shows you how to prepare everything with fresh produce, there are no tins or frozen food here! It encourages you to experiment and try things you may not have heard of before. Fish features strongly here as an alternative to meat dishes, with great new combinations and flavours. It opens the door to a galaxy of sophistication.

Please enjoy reading these recipes – I hope you try some out too. Remember to look out for the freshest vegetables, good quality fish and meat and cook everything with love and affection. Spend a little extra time to present each dish on the plate with care and I assure you that it will make a difference.

In the last chapters of this book I have concentrated Health and Safety and the costing formula with which some caterers and individuals may wish to calculate their spending.

Finally, I would like to offer my thanks to those who have assisted me by reading and commenting on the composition of this book with honesty. I would also like to thank Joy for her patience and practical support. My thanks go also to you, the reader, for your decision to use this book for practical information and to prepare elaborate cuisine. Finally my special thanks go to Jayne and Molly for bringing this book to fruition

Enjoy!

Ali Javaheri

Author's note

Most of the dishes in this book are for 2-8 people, with the exception of snacks, accompaniments, dressings, marinades and party menus, which are presented as batch recipes.

Ingredients are given in both metric and imperial weights. Wines are dry unless otherwise stated and measured in 150ml (1 glass). Butter and olive oil are used in most cases, as are white sugar and plain flour unless you are instructed to use other varieties. Oven temperatures are set at 180°C / 350°F / Gas Mark 4 as standard. All marinated food is marinated for 24 hours and kept in the fridge.

Some of the recipes do not give actual quantities as it depends on how many you are cooking for. Experiment and give yourself a free hand, the more you cook, the more confident you will become.

Cooking Essentials

If I had to start from scratch, my initial requirements would be: vegetable oil, virgin olive oil, malt vinegar, butter, margarine , lemon juice, orange juice, plain flour, Worcester sauce, soy sauce, tomato ketchup, tin plum tomatoes, eggs, cream, milk, sugar, honey, pasta and rice.

Benefits of raw food ingredients

Alfalfa Sprouts and sprouted mung beans - Absorbs cholesterol

Almonds – contains vitamin E and protects the liver cells from free radicals

Artichokes – should be lightly steamed and as they contain Cynarin, they increase the liver's productions of bile. This removes cholesterol from the body and helps to break down fat. They also contain Silymarin which helps new liver cells to grow after excess alcohol consumption.

Aubergines – contains vitamin E and Glutathione, these lessen the absorption of cholesterol from food and help the liver to eliminate environmental toxins.

Beetroot – contains Betaine, a powerful blood cleanser that absorbs homocysteine, which can ravage artery walls and cause heart diseases.

Brazil nuts – contains Selenium and protects cells from environmental toxins.

Chicory – contains Inulin which promotes good bacteria and detoxes the colon.

Broccoli and Cauliflower – contains Sulforaphane and boosts enzymes in the liver that detox the body of pollutants.

Cabbage, Radicchio, Watercress and Pak choi – contains Phenethyl isothiocyanate which absorbs toxins in live and passively inhaled cigarette smoke.

Garlic – contains Alliin whose benefits are antibacterial, antifungal and boosts immunity.

Onions and leeks – contains Sulphur based compounds and Quercetin which reduces cholesterol and is used as an anti inflammatory.

Salad leaves – contains Potassium which lowers sodium and therefore blood pressure.

Tomatoes – contains Lycopene which protects the lungs from pollution.

Sources of nutrients in food

In our day to day life, food plays a major part in our existence. How well and healthy one can live depends upon how much effort one puts into a nutritious diet. The following is an easy to use guide to sources of essential nutrients.

Protein – is essential for the growth of hair, nails and skin and also to maintain the hormones and antibodies to regulate the digestion. Proteins consist of carbon, hydrogen, oxygen and nitrogen. The first class proteins are from animal sources such as meat, milk and eggs. The second class proteins are from vegetables such as wheat, beans, nuts and pulses (lentil, peas, etc).

Vitamins – are essential chemicals required by the body in the form of food. Vitamins fall into two distinct groups: water soluble (vitamin B,C and Folic acid) and fat – soluble vitamins, which are stored in liver and fatty tissues.

A – vitamin A is essential for vision and also keeps the skin and the linings of the stomach, intestines, bladder, throat and respiratory passageways healthy. Recommended daily amount is 750mg.

Sources: parsley, margarine, sorrel, spring cabbage, carrots etc

B – These groups of vitamins are vital to keep the hair, skin, eyes and liver healthy. They are needed for proper functioning of the brain, nervous and circulatory system and for red blood cell formation. The recommended daily intake for this group are as follows:

B1 – 1.5mg; B2 – 1.5mg; B3 – 15-18mg; B6 – 2mg; B12 – 2mg.

Sources: nuts, flour, cheese, egg yolk, mushrooms, bananas.

C – this is necessary for bone cartilage and promotes the healing of wounds and helps the body to fight infection. The recommended daily intake is 30mg.

Sources: lemons, oranges, red peppers, onions, parsley, sorrel, black currants.

D – is an important source of calcium, ensuring the sound formation of bones and teeth. This is especially important for pregnant women and children. The recommended daily intake is 2.5mg.

Sources: brie, cheddar, egg yolks, margarine etc.

E- vitamin E prevents damage to the component of the cell membranes and it protects unsaturated fats in the body from damage. The recommended daily intake is 11mg.

Sources: nuts, egg yolk and margarine.

K- is needed to prevent the body from haemorrhaging. Recommended daily intake is 70-100mg.

Sources: soya beans, cauliflowers, lettuces, cabbages etc.

Folic Acid - for successful formation of genetic materials. The recommended daily intake is 200mg.

Sources: watercress, bran, wheat, yeast extract etc.

Herbs and Spices

You need a mixture of good herbs to give a good flavour and taste to a dish. Every part of the herb can be used: whether seed, flower, bud, leaf, stalk or root; raw, chopped, steamed, blanched or pickled. I like to speak of pot herbs (for bulk in the cooking pot), salet (salad) herbs, sweet herbs (flavouring).

Herbs are cheap, easy to grow and have made their way into household products and cosmetics and provided forms of medical treatment.

Alliums

The most popular allium is the onion family. The Chinese call it the jewel among herbs and vegetables. Alliums are rich in vitamin C and minerals. As for health giving properties, many believe that the stronger the smell, the more effective their healing powers. Pyramid builders and Roman soldiers were given a daily ration of garlic and onion, and today they are a major flavouring in many cuisines. Chives were recorded 4000 years ago in China and they were enjoyed by the traveller Marco Polo. There are many varieties of the onion family and the growth and sweetness differs from country to country. In Spain onions are larger and sweeter in taste, in Mexico they are smaller in size but stronger. Another important allium species in China and Japan is the Welsh onion (Welsh meaning "foreign"). As well as for cooking, onion , chives and garlic are used for medical treatment, decoration and in salads.

Dill

In the old days dill, mint and cumin had a high and sufficiently stable value to be used as tax payment. Before that, the ancient Egyptians had recorded dill as soothing medicine and the Greeks knew dill as the cure for hiccups. In the middle ages, it was one of St John's herbs to be prized as protection against witchcraft. Magicians used dill in their spells and some infused dill in wine to enhance passion. Dill is highly aromatic and has valuable mineral salts including calcium and phosphorus.

As well as its use in cooking, pickles and salads, it is also used in cosmetics. Dill, in the form of dill water, is used for stomach cramps, and indigestion as well as for hiccups.

Tarragon

The term "dragons" is an honour worthy of this culinary herb. The word Tarragon, derives from the French estragon. It was first used to sweeten the breath before it was used in French cuisine. Russian tarragon has a strong flavour, and is normally frozen in ice cubes for flavoured cold drinks. It is used by Persians on grilled meats. It is frequently used in cooking. It is also used to cure toothache and as an appetite stimulant.

Coriander

Coriander was cultivated for some 3000 years for its medicinal use and as a culinary herb. Egyptian's mention it in the Tales of Arabian Nights and in the Bible, where manna is compared with coriander. Romans combined it with cumin and vinegar, rubbed it into meat and used it as a preservative. In the middle ages it was put into love potions. Coriander, with its sweet spicy flavours is used in exotic cuisines. Add essential oil to coriander and rub it onto your skin for painful rheumatic joints and muscles or infuse it in tea for an aperitif.

Mints

In Greek mythology, Menthe was a nymph beloved by Pluto. Mint is a symbol of hospitality. It is highly scented and aromatic with more than 600 varieties. In the old Persia, mint was steamed and the extracts were taken to be used for stomach ache and on some occasions as a cold herbal drink. Many mint varieties have been introduced to Europe since the 9th century. The best way to select a good mint is by nose rather than by name. Mint is used to bring relief from heavy colds, infused as a tea to help digestion, or infused in oil and massaged into the affected areas for migraines or to help muscular aches.

Due to its versatility and aroma, mint is used in decoration, sweet making, flavouring and casseroles.

Basil

Basil, with its warm spicy flavour, sends cooks into a poetic rapture. Basil first originated from India. Indians chose this herb upon which to swear their oaths in court. Some Greek churches used it to prepare the holy water.

With its many varieties, colours and shapes, cooks use it to complement salads and sauces. Some inhale the aroma to allay mental fatigue, other use it for an invigorating bath.

Lemon Balm

Lemon Balm was used by the Greeks some 2000 years ago for medical reasons and was called "hearts delight" in southern Europe, and the "elixir of life" by the Swiss physician, Paracelsus. He believed this herb could completely revive a man, would renew the youth and strengthen the brain. In the 13th century, lemon balm tea was served daily to the prince of Glamorgan "Llewyn", who lived to 108 years. John Hussey, of Sydenham, England lived to 116 after 50 years of breakfasting on lemon balm tea and honey. Today, it is mostly used in aromatherapy to counter depression. Cooks use lemon balm in salads and fish sauces or in cooking poultry and pork. Lemon balm could also be added to fruit salads, or bath water to counter greasy hair.

Marjorams & oregano

The Greeks have given us the legends and the name of this ancient culinary herb: Aros Ganos "joy of the mountain", which covers the hillside of Greece and scents the summer air. Marjoram is known as a symbol of happiness, and bridal couples used to crown themselves with garlands of marjoram. Oregano, is the name given to a wild kind of marjoram and in ancient Egypt, it was used as the antidote to poisoning. Oregano with its power to heal was also used in the middle ages as a disinfectant. Oregano was treasured for its use in cooking roast meats, sauces for pizza, infused as a tea and chopped finely for salads.

Parsley

Romans were the first to use parsley in their food. Greeks used parsley to crown victors at the Isthamian games, decorate tombs and along the edges of herb beds, and also to feed their horses. There are many excellent parsley varieties; Hamburg parsley with flat leaves, English parsley "curled parsley". French use parsley like chervil in their cooking. All parsleys are rich in minerals and vitamins and it is consumed fresh to counter strong breath and promote healthy skin. It is used in sauces by cooks and for decorating and garnishing the plates. Freshly chopped parsley is used for salads, sandwiches and soups.

Sage

"How can a man grow old who has sage in his garden?" is an ancient proverb much quoted in China, Persia and parts of Europe. In the 17th century the Dutch merchants found the Chinese would trade three chests of China tea for one of sage leaves. So, the name "salvia" from the Latin salvere, meaning to be in good health, reflects its reputation. To the Romans it was a sacred herb. This strong culinary herb is often used on its own and as one chef put it: "in the grand opera of cooking, sage is easily offended and likes to have the stage almost to itself". Sage is also used for deodorizing as well as aiding digestion. If sage is taken in infused tea after dinner, it can help with coughs and colds.

Thyme

With its highly strong fragrance, especially on a warm sunny hillside in the Mediterranean, one poet wrote: "a bit of wind thyme smells like the dawn in paradise". To the Greeks, thyme denoted graceful elegance: "to smell of thyme" was an expression of praise. Thymus is derived from the Greek word thymon, meaning courage. Roman soldiers bathed themselves with thyme water and Scottish highlanders drank thyme tea for strength and courage. In cooking it is added to parsley and bay in bouquet garni, but more often it is used on its own in stocks and sauces. Thyme is used for hangovers, and an infusion in honey is good for sore throats. Infused thyme oil is used as a massage for headaches.

Rosemary

"Dew of the sea" holds a special place in any cooks kitchen. It has a reputation for strengthening the memory.   Rosemary became an emblem of fidelity for lovers. Some brides have even worn rosemary wreaths.   The Spanish revere rosemary as the bush that sheltered the virgin Mary on her flight to Egypt. In some Mediterranean villages, linen is spread over rosemary bushes to dry, so that the sun extracts its moth-repellent aroma.   Rosemary is used with a wide range of meat and vegetable dishes, as well as salads and infused in oil.   Rosemary used in food is good specially for blood circulation and boiled in water for ten minutes to yield an antiseptic solution for washing kitchen and bathroom fixtures. It makes a good herb butter and is a good addition for baked potatoes.

Useful spices

Every cook has his own preferences of spices in his kitchen but some of the common spices in every kitchen are as follows:
Salt, pepper, black pepper corn, turmeric, curry powder "mild", paprika, cinnamon, red chillies, dried lime, garlic powder, dried ginger and saffron.

Olive Oil

The nearest parallel to olive oil is wine. Olives are like vines, they take three to seven years to mature.

It is a sad commercial reality that since all the publicity in Britain, United States and Canada about how olive oil is actually good for your health, the massive mass suppliers of Italian, French and Spanish and so many other oil producing regions have to resort to the less traditional system in order to keep their rapidly expanding market. Do not buy cheap olive oil but the most expensive extra virgin olive oil you can afford.

The olive oil of Tuscany is the best known Italian oil. Puglia is the biggest oil producing region in Italy. There can be a distinct difference in oils from estate to estate. When you begin to change regions and type of olives, the changes are so distinct that even the non-expert is quickly capable of telling a Sicilian oil from a Sardinian, Sienna oil from Florence or Ligurian as they all have their own personality and flavour.

So what can you do to make sure you are getting the right oil on your table?

1. Make sure you always buy extra virgin olive oil.
2. Always look for the marking DOP on Italian oil labels. This is the olive growers equivalent of the wine DOC, it stands for Denomination of Origin Protected and it works by the local administrating authorities knowing how many trees are on an estate and then what that year crop levels were like, giving the grower permission to produce a fixed number of DOP oil bottles.

3.   Always look out for single estate oils. That means the grower has gone the extra length to press and bottle his own olives.

4.   Always try to buy oils that have been bottled at the grove rather than the mill.

5.   Don't presume that one olive oil which is good for salad, is good for fish and meat.

Vegetables

Vegetables contain minerals and fibre and are an excellent source of vitamins, particularly vitamin C. Some salad vegetables and some fruit vegetables such as courgettes, aubergines and peppers should be eaten as soon as possible. The polythene wrapping of tomatoes, mushrooms and sweet corn etc, should be removed and kept in a cool dark place. In this condition, carrots and onions will keep longer and potatoes will keep for several weeks, although they do tend to lose their vitamin C content.

Some vegetables are suitable for freezing such as sweet corn, spinach broccoli, carrots, beans and peas but make sure they are blanched for at least one minute in boiling water and completely drained before putting in the freezer.

Root vegetables must be scrubbed and cooked in their skins as most of the flavour and nutrients is in or near the skin. Some vegetables such as artichoke, celeriac and potatoes go brown when cut. To prevent this, drop them in water that has a few teaspoons of lemon juice or vinegar added. It is not important if aubergines go brown, they do not need salt to draw out the water as recommended by some books. For okra, cut off the conical cap at the stalk end, salt and leave for an hour, then rinse dry. For fennel, cut in thin slices and discard the stems and bottom. All other vegetables such as spinach etc must be washed thoroughly. Never cook vegetables in copper or iron pans. Steam vegetables if possible, never overcook. Always make sure the vegetables are barely tender and save the water to make soup.

The following vegetables can be stored in a dark, dry, cold room for up to a week or more: turnips, swede, parsnips, celeriac, sweet potatoes, artichokes, beetroot, asparagus, fennel, onion, leeks, celery, French beans, mange tout, okra, sweet corn, red cabbage, brussel sprouts, cauliflower, broccoli, carrots, potatoes and button mushrooms.

Essential Sauces

The ability to make a good sauce is an asset to any cook. If we give any dish a festive air by dressing it attractively and accompanying it with a tasty sauce, the result is bound to be a success. We just have to make sure the sauce is of a smooth texture and free from lumps. So, we begin by understanding the three main sauces and a number of stocks before we look at the recipes for our sauces.

The three main sauces are:
- Brown sauce
- White sauce
- Red sauce

Brown Sauce

- 1 pint dripping (juice of roast beef)
- 35 ml gravy browning
- 500g flour
- 125g butter
- 2 carrots and 2 large mushrooms, chopped
- 4 - 6 bacon rashers, chopped
- 1 large onion, chopped
- 1 tbsp tomato puree
- 35ml dry sherry

Brown sauces usually range from gravies made from dripping (meat juices), vegetable stock and flour. One variation of brown sauce is known as 'demi glace' and this is made from beef dripping and espanol sauce (butter, chopped bacon rashers, onion, mushroom, carrot, tomato puree, sherry and bouquet garni).

White Sauce

- 250g / 9oz butter or margarine
- 500g / 1lb 2oz flour
- 2 litres 400ml / 4 pints milk
- 4 - 5 cloves
- 1 large onion, quartered
- 1 large carrot, chopped
- 2 celery sticks, chopped
- 4 bay leaves, pinch of salt & pepper

This is the most common type of sauce and is very easy to make. Simply melt the butter or margarine in a pan, add the flour and stir for a minute. Gradually add the milk and bring to the boil, stirring. Simmer for a few minutes to thicken. White sauce also has variations and one of them is known as béchamel sauce, which is made from chopped celery, onion, carrots, cloves and milk. It is brought to the boil, bay leaves are added, then set aside to infuse. It is then strained and added to the white sauce

Red Sauce

- 1kg /A10 tin of peeled, fresh tomatoes, blended
- 1 large onion, finely diced
- 1 clove garlic, finely diced
- 35 ml / 1 ½ fl oz oil
- Pinch of oregano/basil/parsley
- 1 litre / 2 pints water
- 2 tablespoon tomato puree
- 1 tablespoon sugar, pinch of salt & pepper

The red sauce known as tomato sauce is made from peeled fresh or tinned tomatoes, chopped onion, garlic, one tablespoon of sugar, chicken stock (optional), tomato puree, bay leaves and fresh herbs. Once it has simmered and been reduced to a thick sauce, it can be used in many ways, even added to other sauces.

Stock

You need a good stock as well as your main sauces to give a good flavour and taste to a dish. You can buy any stock in the shape of a cube or powder but remember they are generally salty. It is best to make your own stock. Remember that the recipes are similar and can be refrigerated for two days only or can be frozen.

Fish Stock

Ask your fishmonger for any trimmings, bones and skins. Place these in a pan with a knob of butter, 2 tablespoons of flour, some shallots, chopped tarragon, one celery stick and one sliced carrot, with one or two bay leaves. Add 1 litre water and 1 litre white wine with two tablespoons of white wine vinegar, and bring to the boil. Simmer for half an hour, season well and strain.

Beef stock

Ask your butcher for any marrow bones and shin of beef, cut into pieces. Place on a large saucepan with water to cover. Add one large chopped onion, 2 sliced carrots, 2 sliced sticks of celery, 2 whole eggs, a few bay leaves, black peppercorn, a pinch of chopped parsley and a pinch of chopped thyme (or use bouquet garni). Season to taste. Bring to the boil and simmer for approximately 2 hours. Strain and remove all traces of fat.

Chicken stock

For this stock you need a chicken carcass, skins and meat. In a large saucepan put 1 large chopped onion, 1 sliced celery stick, 1 sliced carrot and bouquet garni with a knob of butter. Shallow fry for 1 minute. Add 2 tablespoons of flour and stir for another minute. Place your carcass, skins and meat in the pan and add 3 pints of water, season and bring to the boil. Stir occasionally and simmer for half an hour. Strain in a bowl and remove all the excess fat.

Vegetable stock

Take 1 large chopped onion, 1 chopped leek, 1 chopped celery stick, 1 chopped fennel and 50g of diced cabbage. Wash all your vegetables and place in a saucepan with 2 tablespoons of olive oil. Fry for 2 minutes and add enough water so that it comes one inch above your vegetables (about 2 pints). Add 2-3 cloves and season with salt, pepper and black pepper corns. Bring to the boil and simmer for 30 minutes, then strain.

Remember that you may use this stock in sauces such as béchamel and tomato as well as soups and other sauces.

Fish related sauces
Quick reference

A'l'ail sauce
Known as garlic sauce. Pan fry the garlic and butter, add some lemon juice, salt and pepper to taste.

Admiral sauce
Add to white or German sauce, chopped capers, parsley, anchovy fillet and lemon juice. Bring to boil, add salt to taste.

Anchovy and caper sauce
The same as parsley sauce, but with capers and anchovies.

Béarnaise sauce
Tarragon, white wine vinegar and chopped onion is added to béchamel and brought to boiling point. Add 2 eggs yolks and crushed peppercorn and seasoning to taste.

Citrus fruit
Peel and cut one orange and lemon, fry in butter. Add a glass of sweet white wine or sherry, garnish with the zest of orange and lemon.

Cucumber sauce

Peel the cucumber, cut lengthwise, remove seeds, dice and add to the béchamel sauce. Add dry white wine, cream and seasoning to taste.

Dill sauce
The same as parsley sauce, but with dill.

23

Diplomat sauce

Add to the Normandy sauce crab meat, cut in small pieces and stir in the cream.

Epinard sauce

Fry in butter chopped onion and fresh spinach with a pinch of garlic. Add béchamel and cream. Bring to the boil.

Espagnole sauce

Chopped onion, carrots, mushrooms and bacon should be fried in butter. Add brown stock and pulp tomato. Simmer, strain and reheat.

Florentine sauce

This is exactly the same as epinard sauce.

Hawaiian sauce

Pan fry the chopped seedless apples and pineapple, add honey and white wine, bring to the boil.

Lemon sauce

This is citrus fruit sauce but without orange.

Lobster sauce

Heat the béchamel, add chopped lobster and a pinch of cayenne pepper.

Lyonaise sauce

Put the fish stock, a glass of sherry, some chopped shallots, bay leaf, corn flour and tomato purée into a saucepan. Bring to the boil, add wine and seasoning, sieve and reheat.

Meuniere sauce
Melt butter in the pan, add chopped spring onion, garlic and chopped fresh basil. Shallow fry and add béchamel, cream and white wine.

Minute sauce
Known as hot and spicy. Fry some chopped chillies together with garlic, add Tabasco and soy sauce with tomato and mixed herbs.

Mornay sauce
Peel and dice cucumber, cook with water until puréed. Add aspic jelly, mayonnaise, cream, chopped gherkins and vinegar.

Mustard sauce
Melt the butter, add flour, fish stock and vinegar with French mustard Season with salt and pepper.

Normandy sauce
Melt butter and stir into the flour, add fish stock, egg yolk, lemon juice and season to taste.

Oyster sauce
Remove beards from the oysters and cut into quarters. Melt the butter and add the oyster, béchamel, yolk of egg and lemon juice then heat without boiling and adjust seasoning.

Parquees sauce
A sauce of Dijon mustard, cracked pepper corns, olives, wine vinegar and tomato flavoured with a sprinkle of tarragon.

Parsley sauce
Heat béchamel, add fresh chopped parsley and cream and bring to boil adding a glass of dry white wine.

Poivre vert sauce

This is a pepper sauce with green pepper corns. Fry the chopped onions with green pepper corns in butter, add cream and brandy. Bring to boil, add béchamel to thicken.

Provencale sauce

This sauce can be from the province of anywhere. Panfry the red currants in butter, add red currant jelly and demi– glace with some red wine and rosemary for flavouring.

Puttanesca sauce

This is a sauce made of garlic butter, anchovies, capers and olives with chopped fresh tomato and dry white wine.

Raifort sauce

Heat the horseradish cream with Dijon and lime juice. Add cream and dry white wine, bring to the boil.

Rochealaise sauce

Pan fry the chopped onion in a frying pan with butter, add fish stock, demi– glace and red wine.

Rouille sauce

Pan fry the prawns and olives together with garlic, tomato and mixed herbs. Add dry white wine and salt and pepper to taste.

Tarragon sauce

The same as parsley sauce, but with tarragon.

Tartare sauce

Melt the butter, add chopped onion, gherkins and capers. Stir and add mixed vinegar, mayonnaise and Dijon mustard.

Thermodor sauce
Pan fry finely diced onion and mushrooms in a little butter. Add whole grain mustard and flambé in brandy. Add béchamel sauce and cream and simmer for a few minutes so the sauce reduces. Add salt and pepper to taste.

Watercress sauce
The same as parsley sauce but with chopped watercress.

White mushroom sauce
Cut the mushrooms into thin strips and fry in butter together with finely chopped diced onions. Add béchamel sauce and bring to the boil with cream.

Soups & Accompaniments

Nothing in this world could be simpler than making a soup. All you have to do is to chop a few seasonal vegetables, wash them and put them in a pan with some sort of fat. Add water or stock, season and boil until it is ready to be eaten. The term soup is used for describing a liquid dish ranging from that containing thick chunks of meat to one containing vegetables, herbs and spices.

Some people turn left over food into a sensational soup by blending it. Some soups have a traditional accompaniment such as croutons and grated parmesan cheese. Broccoli and stilton soup is often served with bread dough croutons and shaved parmesan; minestrone soup is served with rice and pasta; lentil soup is often accompanied by bacon. Some soups such as vichyssoise are garnished with chopped fresh herbs (because of their pale colour). Chives, spring onion and fried julienne of leeks all make excellent garnishes.

Soup can be regarded as either a starter or a main course and is extremely nourishing. It contains few boundaries because such a vast variety of ingredients and accompaniments can be used. Soup can be served with either a chunky, rough texture or it can be served smooth by using a blender and sieve. Soups are mainly associated with Winter because they are usually served hot and are considered to be very warming, but why not try a delicious and refreshing cold soup in Summer?

I hope that the selection I have chosen for you will give you an insight into the various types of soups at your disposal, and that it will demonstrate a wealth of flavours and accompanying carbohydrates such as bread, croutons, rice and pasta.

Cream of spiced apple and parsnip soup

serves 8

1 large cooking onion, quartered
3 medium cooking apples, quartered
50g / 2oz root ginger, chopped
250g / 9oz parsnip, roughly chopped
1 tablespoon turmeric
150ml / 5fl oz whipping cream
150g / 5oz flour
125g / 4oz butter
30g / 1oz chicken stock
pinch of mixed herbs

1. Mix the fruit and vegetables together. Bring to the boil with a little water until cooked. Blend until smooth.

2. In a separate pan, melt the butter and add the flour. Stir until brown and add the turmeric and chicken stock. Stir for one minute.

3. Add 2 pints of water and your blended vegetables and reduce by boiling.

4. Add cream and then herbs, simmering for 5 minutes before serving.

Cream of carrot and coriander

Serves 6

500g / 1lb 2oz carrots, peeled and roughly chopped
250g / 9oz onions, peeled and roughly chopped
50g / 2oz fresh ginger, peeled and diced
125g / 4oz butter
250g / 9oz fresh coriander leaves, washed and chopped
150g / 5oz flour
135ml / 4 fl oz single or whipping cream
1 teaspoon crushed black pepper
1 litre / 2 pints chicken stock

1. Place the carrots and onion in a large saucepan with enough water to cover them. Boil for 20 minutes and blend until smoother.

2. In a separate pan, melt the butter and fry the ginger. Add the flour and stir until brown.

3. Add the stock and season with salt and pepper. Bring to the boil and simmer for 5 minutes.

4. Add the cream and coriander, simmer for a further 5 minutes and serve.

Bouillabaisse

Serves 6-8

1kg / 2lb 4oz mixed fish and shellfish
          (i.e. mussels, prawns, monkfish, bass)
3 large onions, sliced
2 garlic cloves, crushed
135ml / 4 fl oz oil
1 celery stick, finely chopped
250g / 9oz fresh tomatoes, peeled, seeded and sliced
pinch saffron strands
rind of 1 orange
1 teaspoon each of dried thyme, fennel and parsley
3 bay leaves
135ml / 4 fl oz white wine

1. Cut the fish into chunks.
2. Place the saffron in 600ml / 1 pint of boiling water and leave to soak for an hour
3. Fry the onion and celery in the oil in a large saucepan until soft. Add the herbs, garlic, tomatoes and orange rind, then add the wine. Season with salt and black pepper and stir for a minute or two.
4. Place the fish in the pan, add the saffron liquid and sufficient water to cover the mixture. Bring to the boil and simmer for 30 minutes
5. Serve immediately with some crusty French bread.

Chinese chicken & sweet corn soup

Serves 4

1 chicken fillet strip
2-3 spring onions, diagonally sliced
1 small red pepper, deseeded and thinly sliced
1 garlic clove, crushed
4 baby sweet corn, diagonally sliced
1 small tin sweet corn
2-3 teaspoons sweet chilli sauce
2 fresh tomatoes, finely sliced
1 cup stock
pinch of fresh coriander, finely chopped
2 tablespoons corn flour
2 tablespoons sweet sherry
2 tablespoons oil

1. Heat the oil in a wok or large pan and fry the chicken until sealed.

2. Add spring onion, peppers, garlic and baby sweet corn and stir for 2 minutes.

3. Add the stock, tinned corn, sherry and chilli sauce and stir for a further 5 minutes.

4. Blend the corn flour with approximately 3 cups of water. Add to the soup and bring to the boil. Add the tomato and coriander and serve immediately.

Minestrone soup

Serves 8

1 leek, sliced

2 carrots, diced

Half a Savoy cabbage, shredded

1 celery stick, diced

1 courgette, diced

3 medium potatoes, diced

1 large onion, chopped
1 garlic clove, crushed

4 tbsp oil

Half a litre / 18 fl oz of beef stock (or made from 1 stock cube)

4 bay leaves and rosemary leaves

3 plum tomatoes, diced

1. Place all vegetables in a pan, add the oil and stir-fry for 2 minutes. Add the stock and season with crushed black pepper and very little salt.

2. Bring 2 litres of water to the boil. Simmer for 30 minutes and add the bay leaves and tomatoes. Simmer for a further 30 minutes.

3. You can add some pasta or beans and simmer for an extra 5 minutes. Serve immediately with Parmesan cheese.

Vichyssoise
(cream of leek and potato soup)

Serves 4

2 leeks , trimmed and sliced

1 medium onion, chopped

350g / 12oz potatoes, sliced

50g / 2oz butter

600ml / 1 pint chicken stock or bouillon (or made from 1 cube)

150 ml / 5 fl oz single cream

2 tbsp chives, snipped

1 tbsp oil

2 bay leaves

1. Place the potatoes in a saucepan with enough water to reach 2 inches above them.

2. When slicing the leeks, save the 2 inches of white head and place the rest in the pan and boil for 10 minutes. Season with a little salt and 2 bay leaves and boil for a further 5 minutes. Drain the water and mix the stock with a blender.

3. In another pan, melt the butter with the onion and stir for 1 minute. Add the flour and stir for another minute. Add 1 pint of water and the cream and pour the blended mixture into the pan with the chives. Simmer to reduce.

4. Serve hot or cold with croutons and crown with fried julienne of leeks.

Lentil & bacon soup

Serves 8

200g / 7oz yellow or red lentils

1 garlic clove, crushed

4 rashers rind less back bacon, diced

500g / 1lb 2oz potatoes, diced

1 can (400g / 14oz) peeled chopped tomatoes

1 medium onion, finely chopped

4 cloves

2 tablespoons lemon juice

2 litres / 4 pints chicken stock

2 tsp turmeric

1. Wash the lentils and place in a large saucepan with the onion, garlic, cloves, bacon and turmeric. Season well and stir for 3 minutes.
2. Add the chicken stock, tomatoes and potatoes and bring to the boil. Simmer for 30 minutes.
3. Add the lemon juice and simmer for a further 5 minutes.
4. Serve hot with croutons or blend until creamy, reheat and serve with chopped parsley.

White haricot bean soup

Serves 6

300g / 12oz haricot beans, soaked overnight
1 cabbage heart
1 medium onion, sliced
500g / 1lb 2oz new potatoes
350g / 12oz leeks, sliced
125g / 4oz butter
1 garlic clove, crushed

1. Soak the beans overnight in a large container of water.

2. In a large pan, glaze the vegetables with butter over a high heat and add 1 litre of water. Season with salt and crushed black pepper, add the beans and simmer gently for about an hour or until the beans are thoroughly cooked. (You may have to add a little water occasionally.)

3. Serve piping hot with French or garlic bread. This soup can be served as a meal on its own. You can also use different types of bean, such as chickpeas, red kidney beans, or butter beans.

French onion soup
(le tourin)

Serves 6

2 Spanish onions (350g / 12oz), thinly sliced

3 large eggs

75g / 3oz flour

125g / 4oz butter

1 beef bouillon cube

3 slices bread, chopped into squares

60g / 2oz shaved or grated parmesan cheese

1. Melt the butter in a large pan and add the onions, stirring until softened.

2. Add the flour and stir for a further minute, seasoning with a little salt and pepper. Add one litre of water and the bouillon cube and simmer gently for 30 minutes. Separate the egg whites from the yolks.

3. Bring a little water to the boil and reduce the heat. Cook the egg whites in the water, drain, and add them to the onion soup.

4. While the soup is simmering, beat the yolks and gradually add them to the pan.

5. Fry the bread cubes in a clean frying pan to make croutons.

6. Serve piping hot, crown with the croutons and some Parmesan cheese. Fresh bread makes a lovely accompaniment.

Potatoes and cooking potatoes

Potatoes are found in nearly every menu category as the main component of appetizers, soups, entrees and side dishes and are one of the most versatile foods. Potatoes are an important ingredient in preparations such as pancakes and breads. Potato varieties differ in starch, moisture contents, skins, flesh colour and shape.

When one goes to the market to choose potatoes, one has to decide what one intends to do with them. The following categories are defined by moisture and starch content. One has to remember, the moisture content of potatoes increases with age and their starch content decreases.

Low moisture / high starch

Includes Idaho and russet potatoes. The higher the starch, the dryer and granular the potato after it is cooked. Those potatoes are perfect for frying and are likely to break and absorb grease. Their low moisture content also makes them perfect for pureeing, baking or for using in casserole style dishes.

Moderate moisture / starch

Includes all purpose potatoes such as red skinned waxy yellow potatoes (Yellow finn, Yukon gold). These potatoes tend to hold their shape after they are cooked. They are perfect for boiling, sautéing, steaming and oven roasting.

High moisture / low starch

Includes any potatoes which are harvested when less than one and a half inches in diameter and known as new potatoes. The skins of these potatoes need not be removed and they are perfect for roasting and boiling.

Baking potatoes with fried onions

Serves 10

10 baking potatoes
285g / 10oz sour cream
2 tablespoons minced chives
285g / 10oz Spanish onions, thinly sliced
60g / 2oz plain flour
60g /1oz corn starch
1 cup olive oil
seasoning

1.   Boil the potatoes whole or bake in a pre heated oven at 220°C / 425°F / Gas Mark 7.

2.   Blend the sour cream and chives, season and keep to one side.

3.   Combine the flour and corn starch, season and add onion, tossing to coat well.

4.   Heat the oil and fry the onions until crisp.

5.   Pinch or cut the potatoes open and place the chives and sour cream on top, crown with the onion.

Baking potatoes en casserole

Serve 10

1.5kg / 3lb 6oz Waxy yellow potatoes
720-900 ml / 24-30 fl oz liquid (milk, stock, sauce)
2-3 egg yolks
115-140g / 4-5oz grated cheese or other toppings
seasoning

1. Slice the potatoes very thinly using a mandolin. Simmer the potatoes before layering in the buttered baking pan.
2. Spread a layer of potatoes, add a layer of cheese, a layer of potatoes then some egg yolk and so on with other toppings if desired. The last layer should be topped with grated cheese and then baked in the oven until cooked through.

Sautéed potatoes

When we talk about potatoes, we have to remember that, each chef from any region or any country has his own unique way of cooking potatoes. Here we only concentrate on the more familiar and most popular way of cooking potatoes and that is to sauté. A combination of browned and crisp exterior with a tender moist interior. The cooking fat plays a significant role in the flavour of the finished dish with vegetable oil, olive oil, butter, lard, goose fat and choices range from home fries, Anna potatoes, potato pancakes, hash browns, rustic, Lyonnaise and Parisian potatoes.

For sautéing; oil, clarified butter, cooking fat or lard are generally used.

Recipes here don't have exact amounts as it depends on how many you are cooking for.

Lyonnaise potatoes – Scrub the potatoes, peel and cut into thick slices. Cook in boiling salted water. Once partially cooked, place in a frying pan with some slices of onions and olive oil or butter. Season well with salt and pepper then fry both sides until golden brown and serve immediately.

Dauphinoise potatoes - Scrub, peel and thinly slice some waxy potatoes. Put them in cold water to stop them discolouring, then drain and dry before cooking. Place the potatoes in a large pan together with milk, salt, pepper and nutmeg, bring to the boil for approximately 15 minutes.
Butter a hotel pan and rub it with a crushed garlic clove. Remove the potatoes from the milk. Blend the 2 eggs into the milk mixture and place a layer of potatoes in the pan. Pour over some of the milk mixture and then spread with a layer of cheese. Repeat until all ingredients are used. Cover and bake in the oven (180°C /350°F / Gas Mark 4) for 45-60 minutes. Uncover during final 10 minutes.

Hash brown potatoes – Scrub, peel and cook the potatoes in a large pan with salted boiling water for 20 minutes. Dry the potatoes in 150°C/300°F/ Gas Mark 2 oven. Slice, grate or dice the potatoes. Heat the oil in a frying pan, add the potatoes and season, then sauté on all sides.

Rissolee potatoes – Also known as **parisienne** potatoes. Scrub and peel the potatoes. Use the parisienne to shape the potatoes and cook in salted boiling water for ten minutes until tender. Spread on a sheet to dry or in a pan on a low heat until the steam has gone and they are dry. Now sauté the potatoes in a pan, on a high heat, then sprinkle with some chopped parsley and serve.

Anna potatoes – Scrub, peel and trim the potatoes to a uniform cylinder shape, then cut into thin slices, using a mandaline. Heat the pan with butter and sauté the potatoes by arranging them in concentric circles. Brush the potatoes with melted butted and wait until the bottom of the potatoes are brown. Turn the potatoes over to the other side which you have just brushed and wait until brown. Place in the oven at 200°C/400°F/Gas Mark 6 for 30 minutes.

Macaire potatoes – Pierce the potatoes in a few place and half cook. Drizzle some olive oil on top and place in the oven (220°C / 425°F / Gas Mark 7) for 1 hour. Scoop out the flesh and fry in the pan with oil.

Rosti potatoes – Scrub and peel the potatoes, then boil in salted water until just tender. Drain, dry and grate on a coarse greater. Fry in oil until golden brown and both sides and serve hot or cold.

Berny potatoes- Scrub, peel and cut the potatoes into large pieces. Place in a pan of salted water and boil until tender enough to mash. Add butter, egg yolks, nutmeg and salt and pepper. Mix well. Combine almonds and breadcrumbs in a shallow container. Shape 60g portions into balls or oblongs, dip in egg and put into almond and breadcrumb mixture. Fry in a frying pan or deep pan fryer. Place on absorbent paper to remove excess oil.

Lorette potatoes- Boil the potatoes until tender then mash. Mix egg yolks with butter, mashed potato and pipe the mixture into crescent shapes on strips of parchment paper. Place in a deep fryer (190°C / 375°F /Gas Mark 5). When the paper has lifted off, dispose of paper and serve when the potatoes are golden brown.

Cooking rice & pasta

The art of cooking pasta

Pasta is cheap, nutritious and very versatile. It can be used as a main dish or as an accompaniment to a main dish. Pasta is basically dough and has hundreds of varieties but we are only familiar with maybe a dozen of them. Pasta comes in dried and pre packed in supermarkets, as pasta secca or as fresh made with spinach (pasta verdi) or made with eggs (pasta uvou) or with tomato (pasta rosso). The dried Pasta is made of wheat (semola di grano duro) and it contains protein, minerals and vitamins. There is also whole-wheat pasta, which is made with flour and consequently tastier.

Cooking pasta

Bring to the boil over a high heat in a large saucepan filled with three quarters water and 2 level teaspoons of salt. Once the water is boiling add three tablespoons of oil and your dried or fresh pasta.

Leave the pan uncovered and stir the pasta with a fork to avoid sticking together for about 2-5 minutes depends on how well you want your pasta to be done. Remove immediately and drain. Wash out the starch with hot water and drain again. Once it is completely drained, put in a container and drizzle some olive oil over it to avoid sticking together. Leave it out uncovered to cool for ten minutes, then cover and refrigerate.

Please remember the life of pasta, as well as rice in the fridge, is only 24 hours. Remember that pasta cannot be frozen, defrosted and micro waved afterwards, unlike rice. Unless it is fresh and can be cooked directly from frozen.

In an Italian restaurant the terms (al'dente) is used for pasta cooked with the bite in it.

Different type of pasta

There is an endless choice in dried or fresh pasta. The most usual types in the super markets are; spaghetti, macaroni, linguine, Tagliatelle, Ravioli, Penne, Rigatoni, Tortellini, Lasagne, Cannelloni and fettucine.

The art of cooking rice

Rice is perhaps the most traditional dish in the world. It is widely used in Asia as part of day-to-day cooking. Depending on the type of grain and its use, there are variations in the available cooking methods.
We are mostly familiar with three types: long grain, medium and short grain. But you may also be familiar with brown rice, which retains its outer bran layer. We generally recognise it as a variety of whole grain. You may also have come across jasmine rice, a wild 'rice' which is not actually rice at all but the seed of an aquatic grass which has a long black grain. The least common variety of rice is that known as 'glutinous' rice, a sticky, sweet, oval, cream-coloured grain used in Chinese cooking. Whatever the type of rice, all contain protein, carbohydrates, minerals and vitamins.
In Persia, rice is cooked in 2 different ways: 1. Chelou 2. Polou. The method of cooking rice in Persia results in a difference in taste and texture from that found in countries such as China, Arabia and Spain, but it has certain similarities with rice cooked in India and Pakistan.

Chelou

Chelou is always served with a meat of some sorts and a thick textured sauce known as khoresht. Chelou is also cooked in 2 different ways; kateh and dami.

serves 4

500g / 1lb 2oz long grain/ basmati rice
1 egg
125g / 4oz butter
3 tablespoons salt

1. Wash the rice thoroughly in cold water. Place in a large pan with salt and plenty of water and bring steadily to the boil. Boil, uncovered for 9-10 minutes, stirring occasionally. Test a few grains by biting them in half to see if they are cooked at the core. For a slightly firmer texture (al dente), less cooking time is needed.
2. When cooked, remove immediately from the heat and drain in a colander. Rinse with lukewarm water to remove the starch.
3. Place 1 tbsp butter and 1 tbsp warm water in a heavy-bottomed saucepan and swirl the pan around to ensure an even coating.
4. Mix the egg yolk with one cup of rice and spread evenly over the bottom of the pan. Fill the pan with the remaining cooked rice and make a deep hole in the centre using the handle of a spoon. Cover for 10 minutes.
5. Remove cover, mix the remaining butter with 3 tablespoons hot water and spread over the top of the rice. Re-cover and leave for a further 20 - 30 minutes. Turn the rice out onto an oval dish, and place the crunchy, crusty base onto a separate dish.

Polou

This rice dish is perhaps one of the most popular one in Persian cuisine. It is made in a similar style as chelou but once the rice is drained it is mixed with vegetables, fruits, meats or nuts. Generous amounts of butter are added and saffron and spices for flavouring. If meat or vegetables are cooked separately, butter is normally mixed with the broth.

Kateh

This rice dish belongs to the northern part of Persia especially on the shores of the Caspian sea. This rice is made in the shape of a cake with no butter or oil added.

500 g / 1lb 2oz of long grain rice
2 tablespoons of oil
1 egg
2 tablespoons of salt

This rice is cooked in the same manner as chelou but its cooking time is more than doubled so that the rice becomes soft. Rinse once and put back in the oiled pan with the lid tightly covered (a cloth could be used to ensure no air escapes) over a low heat for approximately 45 minutes. Remove the pan from the heat and place in the sink in an inch of cold water for ten minutes. To serve, simply turn the pan upside down to have the crunch on top of your cake shaped rice.

Dami

Dami is the fast way of making chelou. Cover the rice with one inch of water. If you are using 500g of rice add one teaspoon of salt and three tablespoons of butter and cover tightly to boil and wait until all the water has disappeared. Remove the lid. Add three more tablespoons of butter mixed with warm water and put the lid back on for another thirty minutes. Serve the same way as you serve the chelou.

Boiled

This method of cooking is mainly used in Chinese and Indian cooking. It is the fastest way of cooking rice. Use 6 pints of water per 500g rice. Bring to the boil, add one level tablespoon of salt and leave the pan uncovered for 15 minutes until the rice is tender. Remove the pan, drain and rinse with hot water and drain again. Separate the grains with a fork and serve immediately. Please note that for brown rice you have to double the boiling time.

Broad bean and dill rice

Serves 4

500g / 1lb 2oz basmati rice
500g / 1lb 2oz fresh broad beans
100g / 3 ½ oz dried or 350g / 12oz freshly chopped dill
125g / 4oz butter
1 Pita bread
1 tablespoon vegetable oil
1 teaspoon saffron strands
Pinch of salt

1. Prepare the saffron strands by soaking in a cup of boiling water for 30 minutes.

2. Squeeze each broad bean so that the skin breaks and the bean pops out.

3. Bring the rice to the boil in a large saucepan with a pinch of salt and simmer, adding the beans and dill, until half cooked. Rinse with boiling water and drain.

4. Drizzle the oil and half a cup of water into a large saucepan with a little salt. Cut open the pita bread and place at the bottom of the pan.

5. Gradually place the rice in the saucepan (forming a pyramid) on a low heat, for 45 minutes.

6. Make a few holes in the rice and place the butter over it in small pieces.

7. Serve immediately, with saffron sprinkled over. An ideal accompaniment to any lamb stew or roast.

French beans and tomato rice with lamb

Serves 4

500g basmati rice
250g / 9 oz can French beans cut in one cm lengths
1 medium onion finely diced
250g / 9oz lamb shoulder cut in to one cm pieces
1 tablespoon turmeric
1 teaspoon crushed garlic
125g / 4 oz chopped tomato
1 tablespoon tomato purée
Pinch salt and pepper
1 tablespoon lemon juice
3 tablespoon oil
1 pita bread

1. Boil the rice until half cooked then wash under warm water and drain well.

2. Fry the onion, garlic and meat, tossing as you go along and adding the turmeric and seasoning.

3. Add chopped tomatoes and a little water with tomato purée and lemon juice.   Simmer on a low heat until the sauce is reduced.

4. Add the French beans to the sauce (if you are using the ready cooked can) and simmer for one more minute.

5. Using a large saucepan on a high heat, add oil and half a cup of water and season. Cut open the pita bread and lay it at the bottom of the pan and lower the heat. Place a layer of rice and a layer of sauce alternately until you have formed a pyramid.   Close the lid tightly and leave on the heat for 45 minutes.   Serve immediately.

Risotto Ai Frutti Di Mare
(seafood rice)

Serves 4

500g / 1lb 2oz Risotto / short grain rice
4 anchovy filets
125g / 4 oz tuna chunks
125g / 4oz Dublin bay prawns
125g / 4oz shelled mussels
1 clove garlic, crushed
1 medium onion, finely diced
75g / 3oz butter
135 ml / 4 fl oz white wine
125g / 4 oz / 2-3 fresh tomato, finely diced

1.   Place the rice in a large sauce pan, cover with water 2 inches
      above the rice and bring to the boil for a few minutes until the
      rice is al dente (has a bite in it).

2.   Remove from the heat, wash and drain under the warm tap and
      then return the rice to the saucepan.

3.   Place the butter in a frying pan together with the garlic and fish,
      and stir for 2 minutes until all the juice has evaporated. Season
      well.

4.   Add the wine or fish stock and tomato and let it simmer on a low
      heat until the sauce is reduced.

5.   Transfer the contents of the frying pan to the rice and stir on a
      low heat for 2 minutes. Serve immediately.

Vegetarian Risotto

Serves 4

500g / 1lb 2oz risotto rice / short grain rice
1 medium onion, finely chopped
1 celery stick, finely diced
1 small red pepper, finely diced
40g / 2oz button mushrooms, sliced
1 clove garlic, crushed
4 head of spring onion, cut diagonally in small pieces
30g / 1 ½ oz pitted black olives
225g / 8 oz / 3-4 freshly chopped tomatoes
3 tablespoons of oil

1. Bring the rice to the boil with a little salt until half cooked. Wash and dry under warm water, drain and place back in the saucepan.

2. Place all the vegetables in a pan with oil and toss until softened. Add tomato and season well and simmer on a low heat to reduce the sauce.

3. Transfer the sauce to the saucepan and mix the rice with the sauce over a low heat.   At this stage, adding some chopped fresh tarragon or basil or one or two splashes of white wine would be an option.

Pasta Carbonara

Serves 4

250g / 9oz dried / 800g / 1lb 12 oz cooked pasta
4-6 bacon rashes, cut roughly
2 teaspoon crushed garlic
Knob of butter
4 egg yolks
150g / 5oz mushrooms, finely sliced
2 tablespoons grated Parmesan cheese
Pinch chopped parsley
270 ml / 9 fl oz / 2 glass whipping cream
1 teaspoon crushed black peppercorn

1. Place butter, garlic, mushrooms and bacon in a frying pan. Stir and toss for 2 minutes.

2. Reheat the cooked pasta in a microwave or blanch in boiling water for 10 seconds and drain. Add the pasta to the frying pan, season and toss over the heat.

3. In a separate bowl, beat the yolks together with half the Parmesan and cracked black pepper, mix well. Add the cream and mix again.

4. Pour the mixture into the pasta, toss and serve immediately before the eggs turn into lumps. Sprinkle the Parmesan over the pasta and garnish with chopped parsley.

Butter bean linguini

Serves 4

800g / 1lb 12oz cooked/ 250g / 9oz dried linguini pasta
1 large courgette, thickly sliced
1 yellow pepper, roughly chopped
1 garlic clove, crushed
225g / 8 oz (one can butter beans)
270 ml / 9 fl oz / 2 glass whipping cream
2 egg yolks
50g / 2oz grated Parmesan cheese
50g / 2oz shaved Parmesan
1 teaspoon cracked black pepper
Knob of butter

1. Place the butter with garlic, peppers and courgettes in the frying pan and toss them until softened.

2. Drain the butter beans and add to the sauce. Keep it on a low heat.

3. Reheat the pasta in a microwave or blanch in hot boiling water for ten seconds Remove and drain, then add to the frying pan and toss.

4. Beat the egg yolks, season with a little salt and cracked black pepper. Mix in all the cream and add to the pasta and toss. Serve immediately with some freshly shaved Parmesan cheese.

Artichoke and tomato pasta

Serves 1

200g / 7 oz cooked pasta
30g / 1oz diced onion
30g / 1oz black olives
30g / 1oz sliced mushrooms
30g / 1oz mixed pepper
30g / 1oz tomato, cubed
30g / 1oz olive oil
60g / 2oz artichoke
135 ml / 4 fl oz white wine/water (optional)
Pinch salt and cracked black pepper

1. Heat the olive oil in the wok or the frying pan, add onion and peppers, tossing them for a minute or so.

2. Add your mushrooms, olives and artichoke, toss for another minute.   Add tomatoes and a glass of white wine and simmer to reduce the sauce. Adjust seasoning.

3. Heat the pasta in the microwave or by putting it in boiling water for ten seconds and drain.

4. Place the pasta in the centre of a large bowl. Place sauce on top of the pasta.

5. This dish is normally served with shaved Parmesan cheese and garnished with a fresh basil leaf.

Chicken and spinach pasta

Serves 1

200g / 7oz cooked pasta
125g / 4 oz / Half chicken fillet pieces
75g / 3oz baby spinach
One tablespoon chopped onion
One teaspoon chopped garlic
50 ml / 2 fl oz / less than half glass chicken stock
Splash white wine
30 ml / 1 fl oz double cream
40g / 2oz shaved Parmesan
Pinch salt and cracked black pepper
Knob butter

1. Heat the pasta in the microwave or by dipping it into boiling water and drain.

2. Fry the strips of chicken in butter, add onion and garlic tossing it as you go along. Add spinach, stock, wine and cream. If necessary add a little water. Season well and simmer to reduce.

3. Place your pasta in a large bowl, pour the sauce over the pasta and crown it with Parmesan cheese. Sprinkle with some chopped parsley to garnish

Seafood pasta

Serves 4

800g / 1lb 12oz cooked pasta/ 250g / 9 oz dried pasta
100g / 3 ½ oz cockles, shelled
100g / 3 ½ oz mussels, shelled
200g / 7oz squid, ringed
4 fillets of anchovies
100g / 3 ½ oz cocktail cooking prawns
One clove garlic, crushed
225g / 8 oz can chopped tomato or 4 fresh tomatoes, finely chopped
Knob of butter
135 ml / 4 fl oz white wine
salt & pepper
basil (optional)

1. Place the butter in a frying pan together with the garlic.

2. Add all the fish to the pan, stir and toss over a low heat.

3. Season well, add chopped tomatoes and wine and let it reduce on a low heat. Add a pinch of chopped fresh basil (optional).

4. Heat the pasta in the microwave or in boiling water, making sure the water is totally drained.

5. Place the pasta in a large bowl and cover it with the sauce. Garnish with fresh basil leaves and serve with garlic bread.

Penne All' Arabiata

Serves 4

100g / 3 ½ oz streaky bacon, chopped into small pieces
200g / 7 oz button mushrooms, sliced
400g / 14 oz chopped fresh tomatoes
50g / 2 oz butter
1 clove of garlic, finely chopped
50g / 2 oz grated Parmesan cheese
1 teaspoon dried chilli pepper
1 tablespoon dried or Pinch of freshly chopped basil
500g / 1 lb 2 oz dried or 800g / 1 lb 12 oz cooked penne pasta

1. In a large frying pan or saucepan, place the butter, bacon, mushrooms and garlic and stir for a minute or two. Season well with salt and pepper and chilli peppers.

2. Add the chopped tomatoes to the pan with a little water and reduce the sauce.   Add basil and Parmesan and stir over a low heat.

3. Heat the pasta and add it to the pan, stir well and serve immediately.

Spaghetti bolognaise

Serves 4

800g / 1lb 12 oz cooked spaghetti or 250g / 9 oz dried
750g / 1lb 7oz minced beef (lean)
1 large onion, finely diced
1 clove of garlic, crushed
2 tablespoon oil
1 tablespoon tomato purée
1 can or 225g / 8 oz chopped tomatoes
1 tablespoon or 1 stick of cinnamon
1 glass or 135 ml / 4 fl oz red wine
4 bay leaves

1. Place the minced beef, onion and garlic in a large sauce pan over a high heat and stir until the meat has turned brown.

2. Add tomatoes, a little water, wine, cinnamon stick, bay leaves, tomato purée and season well. Leave it to simmer over a low heat for 20 minutes.

3. Heat the pasta and place it in the middle of a large bowl, spoon out the sauce over the pasta.

4. This is best served with grated Parmesan cheese and a slice of garlic bread.

Lasagne Verdi Al Forno

Serves 8

500g / 1lb 2oz dried lasagne sheets ready to cook
100g / 3 ½ oz grated cheddar cheese
4 boiled eggs, finely chopped
4 rashes of bacon, grilled and chopped into pieces
1 litre / 35 fl oz tomato sauce
1 litre / 35 fl oz béchamel sauce
500g / 1lb 2oz bolognaise

1. In a medium size ovenproof dish, spread some tomato sauce. Cover the sauce with a layer of lasagne, horizontally so that the edges touch each other. Cover the sheets with some béchamel.

2. Cover that layer with chopped eggs. Add a layer of lasagne, this time vertically. Cover the sheets with bolognaise and chopped bacon. Add a layer of lasagne horizontally and cover with béchamel and grated cheese. Add a layer of lasagne vertically and cover with tomato sauce and some béchamel and the remaining grated cheese.

3. Cover the dish with foil shiny side down. Place the dish in the pre-heated oven 180°C /350°F / Gas Mark 4 for 20-30 minutes.

4. After the lasagne has cooled down at room temperature it can be portioned and frozen.

Pastry

You don't have to be a chef to make a good pastry, but there are some simple rules that you can't ignore. Frozen pastry can be purchased from the large super stores and is as good as homemade. Chefs and cooks do not waste their time making pastry as it needs expertise and patience. It is an art in itself especially if making pastry for desserts. I only use pastry casings to slide into the mould for making pates or quiches.

Pastry Base

1kg / 2lb 4oz plain flour
500g / 1lb 2oz butter
20g / 1oz salt
1 egg
cup of water

1. Mix all the ingredients thoroughly to shape a ball, flatten it by using a rolling pin. Dust the dough generously with flour.
2. Roll out and fold it in half to form a pocket slightly bigger than your mould. Use the rolling pin to open the pocket and shape it inside your mould using your fingers. I normally use dough that has been made the day before or frozen sheets of ready made pastry.
3. When the pastry fits into the mould evenly and completely, use a pair of scissors to cut off the excess pastry leaving half an inch above the mould for crimping and decorating.

Short Pastry

Short pastry has a variety of uses in any kitchen and can be made in no time. There are two types of short pastry, one of which is known as pate brisee which is made with sugar. Chefs use it for making tarts and pies. The other kind is known as pate a foncer in which sugar is not used. Cooks use this for making turnovers and dumplings.

1 whole egg
250g / 9oz plain flour
150g / 5oz butter
20g / 1oz / 4 tablespoons sugar
pinch of salt
water

1. Make a well in the centre of the flour, break the egg into it and mix well.

2. Add butter, sugar and salt, then start mixing and kneading. Add a little water a bit at a time until a smooth paste has developed.

3. Flatten with the palm of the hand. Let it sit for 30-40 minutes before use.

Pancakes

In this section you will realise how easy it is to make batter for pancakes to be used for light bites and puddings, this is called pouring batter. The other batter, known as coating batter, is thicker and is used for deep frying. There are variations to everything we make and pancakes are no exception. One of the variation is known as crepes Suzette.

Batter

1 litre / 35 fl oz milk
8 egg yolks
100g / 3 ½ oz plain flour

1.   Place the egg yolks in a bowl and mix well.

2.   Add the flour, mix well using a whisk. Gradually pour in the milk whisking the contents until you achieve an even consistency.

Flour Pancake

Serves 8

100g / 4oz plain flour
1 egg, beaten
300ml / ½ pint milk
vegetable oil
pinch salt & pepper

1. Sift the flour, salt and pepper into a large bowl, mix well and make a well in the centre.

2. Add the beaten egg and gradually pour in the milk while mixing to form a batter.

3. Heat a little oil or brush the frying pan with oil and heat on a low setting. Pour off any surplus.

4. Pour in just enough batter to cover the base of the pan and cook until golden brown. Turn and toss, then cook the other side.

5. Spread a clean cloth over the working surface and transfer the pancake onto the cloth in order to cool down.

6. Pile the pancakes on top of each other, with greaseproof paper between each one.

Crepe Suzette

50g / 2oz butter
25g / 1oz caster sugar
35ml orange flavoured liqueur
35ml brandy or rum
finely grated rind and juice or 1 large orange
8 freshly cooked pancakes
cream

1. Melt the butter in a large frying pan then remove from the heat. Add sugar and orange rind.

2. Add the orange juice and the liqueur. Heat gently to dissolve the sugar.

3. Keep the pan on a very low heat and fold each pancake twice to form a fan shape and place in the frying pan in overlapping lines.

4. Pour the brandy over the pancakes and set it alight.

5. Serve at once with fresh cream.

Crepe butter

Serves 6   quantity 12

Making crepe butter is as easy as a pancake and it only takes a few minutes. This is a fine finish to any dinner table.

250g / 9oz plain flour
2 tablespoons butter
6 eggs
6 tablespoons caster sugar (super fine)
3 cups of milk
zest of 1 lemon
3 tablespoons Dark rum

1.   Sift the flour into a large bowl. Melt the butter, add a pinch of salt, break in the eggs and add the sugar.

2.   Stir the ingredients until smooth, pour the milk in and stir, then add the lemon zest and rum and mix well with a whisk.

3.   Lightly butter a frying pan with a brush, only for the first few crepes.

4.   Let the batter rest for at least an hour or in the fridge for a day or two.

Pizza

A pizza is made with bread dough and spread with a zesty tomato sauce and cheese. The ingredients are mounted separately on top of one another. Pizza's originally came from Italy but they are popular world wide. The dough for a pizza needs a lot of kneading and is baked in a hot oven. They have a life expectancy of one or two days in a refrigerator. Pizza's are perfect as a light meal and can be used for parties and buffets.

Useful tips for making a pizza:

Make sure that the dough is made at least a day earlier
The dough is rolled out and left in a room temperature.
Grease the pan with a brush in order to have a nice crust.
Try to make an edge using your finger.
Spread a layer of tomato sauce but not too much to make it soggy.
Cut your vegetables very fine.
Make sure the meat is precooked.
Avoid too many toppings.
Use pitted olives and boneless fish such as prawns, tuna and anchovies.
Sprinkle a layer of cheese or slices of cheese after the tomato sauce has been added, or as a final topping.

Pizza Base

1.5kg / 3lb 6oz plain flour
1 cup of oil
125g / 4oz yeast
2 tablespoons salt
1 tablespoon white sugar
1 litre / 35 fl oz water

1. Mix the salt, sugar, oil and yeast in the warmed water.
2. Make a big hole in the flour and gradually pour the water in the hole and mix using your hand until all the flour is mixed, giving you a very thick smooth creamy texture.
3. Depending on the size of your pizza pans, make balls accordingly. For the plate size, make 200g balls for thin pizzas and 350g for deep pan pizzas.
4. Make sure you dust your hands with flour so the dough will not stick. Once you have made the balls, leave them on a flat surface in room temperature. Make sure the balls are totally covered with a cloth or plastic for 20 minutes in order for the yeast to work.
5. Then roll them out keeping the round shape. Wrap them in cling film and freeze if using at a later date or half cook at 180°C /350°F / Gas Mark 4, then refrigerate.

Quiches

Quiches are described as pies. In France, Canada and Switzerland, they are known as flamiches or crustades. Quiches have so many things in common with pizza's. They both have crusty bottoms, are filled with a variety of ingredients, they contain cheese and are baked in ovens.

The quiche base is made with puff pastry and filled with savoury custard combined with ingredients and cheese. They originated in the Alsace-Lorraine region of France and are popular worldwide. Due to their versatility, shape and ingredients, they reflect the imagination of the chef. Life expectancy is between one and two days in a refrigerator.

The main ingredients are bacon and ham. The type of cheese is normally Swiss cheese which is bound with a custard, made of honey, cream, milk, eggs, nutmeg and seasoning.

Custard	Fillings	Pastry
1 cup of milk	knob of butter	one sheet of puff pastry
1 cup of cream	100g Swiss cheese	or 200g home made
4-5 eggs	100g bacon	
1 teaspoon nutmeg	100g Honey roast ham	

Cooking time – 30 minutes

Beat the eggs in a large bowl, season with nutmeg. Add a little salt and pepper, then the milk and cream.

Fry the chopped bacon, then wash and dry to reduce the fat content.

Add chopped cooked ham and grated Swiss cheese. Make sure you mix everything well.

Slide the puff pastry into the mould for the quiche, making sure it is 1cm larger than your mould. Pinch the excess pastry with your fingers to shape.

Pre-cook the pastry on a low heat in the oven for about 20 minutes. Put the ingredients into the quiche & cook until done.

Ballotines

The term ballotine is used for individual portions unlike galantine which is used for large preparations. There are a lot of similarities in the preparation of ballotine and galantine. No moulds are used and they are never wrapped in any kind of pastry. They are both poached in the liquid stock which compliments them. The preparation of the ingredients is more or less the same.

We use small birds for ballotines and stuff them, unlike galantines, then we use skins.

This can be time consuming but a delicious dish with so many ingredients and so much flavour.

Guinea fowl, squab and quail are perfect birds for ballotines and in order to stuff them you must cut along the breast, leaving the wings and the leg.

Once you open the bird, place your stuffing in the middle, close and sew back the skin to keep the shape of the bird, before poaching them.

Ballotines are served as starters, normally with some crisp leaves and melba toast.

Galantine

The term Galantine is used for large preparations as in Ballotine. It is served as a starter in restaurants but mainly for party buffets. Once you know how galantine is made, you can change the ingredients according to your taste. Here, I include my favourite recipe for you.

La Galantine De Volaile De Olive
(Chicken Galantine)

1.5-2kg / 3lb 6oz-4 ½ lb whole chicken (ask the butcher to remove the bone, leaving the skin all in one piece)
225g / 8oz pork sausages, sliced
150g / 5oz pitted olives, whole
225g / 8oz jambon or smoked bacon, chopped
125g / 4oz butter
50g / 2oz Pistachio nuts, whole
1 clove garlic, crushed
135 ml / 4 fl oz white wine
100g / 3 ½ oz foie gras

Put all the meat in a blender with the foie gras and half the white wine (brandy optional) and mince. Place the contents into a bowl and add the olives and nuts.
Place the mixture in the cavity of the chicken skin with the butter and roll, then sew up the neck tail and along the back with a needle and thread and you end up with a salami shaped sausage. Wrap tightly in cling film and tie up with string as if it was a joint of meat.
Place the wrap in a big ovenproof dish. Place the marrow bones around it with the rest of the wine and a little water. Cover with foil.
Place in the oven on a low heat for an hour. Remove and cool at room temperature, then place in the fridge for 24 hours.
Slice to serve with some chopped jelly on a bed of crisp leaves and melba toast.

Terrines

The term terrine is normally associated with a smooth texture. Terrines are very popular starters in France and most European countries. Terrines are served with melba toast and could be used for large parties in finger buffets by simply spreading on a cracker. My favourite recipe is chicken liver terrine but every chef uses his or her own ingredients:

Place the liver, bacon, garlic and onion in a blender to mince. Add butter, eggs, red wine, cream and seasoning and blend again for a few seconds.

Transfer the contents into a greased non stick loaf tin and then place in an oven dish or roasting pan. Add enough water to come halfway up the loaf tin and then place in an oven at150°C /300°F / Gas Mark 2 for an hour. Remove and place a weight on top of the loaf tin over night. Roll out the pastry onto a floured surface. Turn the pâté upside down and encase in the pastry. Trim, decorate and glaze.

Place on a baking sheet in a roasting pan and bake in the oven for 30 minutes. Remove and cool on a wire rack then serve sliced with melba toast.

Gelatine & aspics

Jellies are made with gelatine powder and gelatine leaf. Four sheets of leaf gelatine are equivalent to 15ml or one tablespoon of powdered gelatine. When using powdered gelatine always add the gelatine to the liquid over a very low heat. The gelatine must not be allowed to boil. For leaf gelatine, snip and soak the gelatine in liquid for 10 minutes before dissolving in the same way as powdered gelatine. Agar-agar can be used as a setting agent and can be obtained from major supermarkets and health food stores.

Aspics are a lovely addition to a dinner buffet. Aspics can be made in several shapes by using different moulds and the ingredients can vary to reflect the season and the taste of the chef. All the ingredients can be seen through the clear aspic, it is important that we shape our ingredients in an attractive way. The aspic you make must be of a firm texture to enable you to cut through it. The aspic colour should be appetizing amber and should be crystal clear. Fish stock is used for seafood and vegetable stock for meat or vegetables. You may use different colours for assembling the aspic. Once aspic is made, it should be left in the mould and covered securely with cling film and refrigerated. My favourite aspic is chicken aspic with sherry. Please refer to Aspic Mould.

Claret Jelly

Serves 4

300ml / ½ pint water or strawberry juice
300ml / ½ pint claret
50g / 2oz sugar
juice & finely grated rind of ½ a lemon
20ml / 4 teaspoons gelatine powder
colouring

Bring all the ingredients to a simmering point over a low heat, strain through muslin and add colouring. Pour into a wetted mould, cool and refrigerate for several hours.

Chicken aspic with Sherry

for 2 litre / 2 quart moulds

1 large chicken
3 carrots
1 stalk celery
1 large onion
30g / 1oz shallots
3 cloves garlic
1 Bouquet garni
9 quail eggs
30g / 1oz corn kernels
50g / 2oz green beans
75g / 3oz peas
100g / 3 ½ oz turnips
truffles
chicken aspic
135ml / 4 fl oz sherry

Refer to aspic mould for basic method

Aspic mould

Use the right gelatine, prepare the garnishes carefully and attractively.
Aspic moulds can be made individually or large enough to serve
several people. They can be made in metal moulds to be unmoulded
for presentations or plastic moulds can be used which allow the
ingredients to be visible.
For these recipes, we are using aspic for several people.

Aspic mould with Vegetables & Basil

Serves 6

45g / 1 ½ oz green beans
100g / 3 ½ oz peas
45g / 1 ½ oz carrots
45g / 1 ½ oz sweetcorn
45g / 1 ½ oz zucchini
1 small bunch of basil
6 quails eggs (optional)
2 ½ cups of aspic

1. Peel and cut the vegetables into small pieces, cook in salted boiling water until firm (not crunchy). Dip the vegetables in iced water and drain.

2. Pour the aspic followed by a layer of vegetables. Wait for the aspic to set after each alternative layer. Place the eggs if using in the centre of the mould, which makes the mould look attractive when it is cut open. Ensure the julienne of basil is 'fluffed up' so that it can be evenly distributed throughout the mould.

3. Fill the mould to the rim with the aspic. Chill to set.

4. Unmould and plate the aspic in the manner appropriate to their presentation.

La Terrine de Foie de Volaile
(Chicken Terraine)

9oz / 250g chicken liver, cut into small pieces
9oz / 250g pork sausages, sliced
9oz / 250g stewing veal, cut into pieces
1 clove garlic, crushed
1 large onion, diced
3 bay leaves
1 egg
35ml / 2 tablespoons brandy
135 ml / 1 glass white wine
125g / 4 oz butter

1. Place all ingredients, except butter, with a little water in an ovenproof dish. Cover with foil, shiny side down and place in oven for approximately 45 minutes. Remove, cool down at room temperature.

2. Mince all the ingredients in a blender and transfer to a large bowl. Melt the butter and add to the bowl. Season well and mix.

3. Wrap the roll in cling film to give you a sausage shape.

4. Refrigerate for at least 24 hours before serving. This is normally served with melba toast and salad garnish.

Pâté en Crute (Chicken liver pâté)

Pâté is a kind of terrine. En crute means enclosed in a pastry casing which can be made into any shape. The casing can contain any filling or ingredients including meat, fish, poultry and vegetables with carefully selected seasonings and garnishes. This is then baked in the oven. The flavour is further enhanced when served, with marinades, marmalades and sauces that marry well with the taste of all the other ingredients.

450g / 1lb chicken liver, trimmed and cut into small pieces
100g / 3 ½ oz bacon rashers, chopped
1 large onion, chopped
1 clove garlic, crushed
125g / 4oz butter
4 eggs
135ml / 4 fl oz double cream
135ml 4 fl oz red wine
1 sheet Puff pastry or 350g / 12 oz short crust pastry
3-4 bay leaves
pinch cracked black pepper
seasoning

1. Place the liver, bacon, garlic and onion in a blender to mince. Add butter, eggs, red wine, cream and seasoning and blend again for a few seconds.
2. Transfer the contents into a greased non stick loaf tin and then place in an oven or roasting pan. Add enough water to come half way up the loaf tin and then place in the oven and cook for 1 hour at 150°C /300°F / Gas Mark 2.
3. On a floured surface, roll out the pastry, turn the pate upside-down and encase it in the pastry. Trim, decorate and glaze.
4. Place on a baking sheet in a roasting pan and bake in the oven for 30 minutes.
5. Remove and cook on a wire rack then serve with melba toast.

Salads

Peri Peri Chicken Salad

1 chicken breast, marinated for 24 hours in peri peri sauce
125g / 4 oz mixed lettuce leaves
8 red onion rings
40g / 1 ½ oz Sundried tomato peri peri dressing

1. Cook the marinated chicken breast on the char grill or under a salamander. Place the mixed leaves in the bowl.
2. Slice the chicken breast diagonally and place above the leaves.
3. Place the onion rings on top of the chicken and drizzle the dressing over the rings.

Caesar Salad

140g / 5 oz Cos lettuce
50g / 2oz Caesar dressing
100g / 3 ½ oz croutons
50g / 2 oz shaved Parmesan cheese

1. Place the cos lettuce in a pasta bowl, drizzle over the dressing.
2. Toss the salad, distribute the croutons around it and sprinkle Parmesan over it.

Salad Nicoise

1 tuna steak or 225g / 8oz can of tuna in brine
1 hard boiled egg, quartered
20g / 1 oz black olives, pitted
50g / 2oz / 2 boiled new potatoes, quartered
2 anchovy fillets
20g / 1oz capers
50g / 2oz green beans, cooked
25g / 1oz / 1 fresh tomato, quartered
20g / 1oz red onion rings, sliced
100g / 3 ½ oz mixed leaves
50g / 2 oz bread dough, baked
3 tablespoons French dressing

1. Place the leaves in a pasta bowl or on a large plate. Add olives, capers and beans.

2. Place the tuna on top of the salad. Place the onion rings on top of the tuna and anchovy on top of the onion rings.

3. Arrange the tomato, bread dough, egg and potatoes around it.

4. Drizzle the dressing over the salad and serve.

Salad Olivet

125g / 4oz / ½ chicken breast, boiled and chopped
2 potatoes, boiled and mashed
1 egg, hard boiled and diced
20g / 1oz cooked peas
20g / 1oz carrot, freshly grated
25g / 1oz green pitted olives, chopped
25g / 1oz gherkins, diced
3 tablespoons mayonnaise
juice of ½ a lemon
½ clove garlic, crushed
seasoning

1.   Place all the ingredients in a very large bowl and mix well.

2.   Season and serve on a bed of mixed leaves with some lemon
     wedges and French or hot pita bread.

Greek salad

2 fresh tomatoes, cut into chunks
1 green pepper, seeded and thinly sliced
½ cucumber, thickly sliced
50g / 2oz pitted olives
150g / 5 oz feta cheese, diced
120 ml / 4 fl oz olive oil
juice of ½ a lemon

1.   Place all the ingredients in a bowl and mix.

2.   Add oil and lemon juice, season well and serve with hot pita bread.

Coleslaw

¼ white cabbage, shredded
½ carrot, grated
½ large onion, chopped finely
2 celery sticks, finely sliced
100g / 3 ½ oz mayonnaise

1.   In a large bowl, combine all the ingredients and toss well.

2.   Refrigerate for freshness and serve on its own or with jacket potatoes or as a garnish.

Seafood salad

Serves 12 as starters / 6 as main course

500g shelled cooked mussels
1 medium onion, roughly chopped
225g / ½ lb Dublin bay prawns, thawed and thoroughly dried if frozen
225g / ½ lb scallops, shelled
225g / ½ lb squid, cleaned and ringed
30g / 2 tablespoons capers
2 small mixed peppers, cored, seeded and finely sliced into strips
1 medium carrot, peeled and grated
150ml / 5 fl oz olive oil
70 ml / 3 fl oz freshly squeezed lemon juice
3 tablespoons chopped parsley
1 clove garlic, crushed
6 pitted black olives, halved

1. Place some water in a large saucepan, season with salt & pepper, add onion and bring to the boil.

2. Cook the prawns, mussels, scallops and squid for 3 minutes in the boiling water and set aside.

3. Reduce the boiling water to a minimum and let it cool.

4. Mix the capers, oil, lemon juice, parsley, carrots, olives, peppers and garlic in a separate bowl.

5. Add the reduced sauce to the mixed dressing bowl and pour over the seafood, season well and toss before serving.

Shiraze Salad (minced salad)

Serves 6 as a side order

1 small iceberg lettuce, finely diced
6 heads of spring onions, finely diced
3 medium tomatoes, finely diced
½ cucumber, peeled and finely diced
30g / 1 oz olives, pitted and diced
1 celery stick, trimmed and finely diced
1 medium red pepper, seeded and diced
6 radishes, finely diced
30g / 2 tablespoons fresh coriander, finely chopped
3 tablespoons virgin olive oil
3 tablespoons freshly squeezed lemon juice
3 tablespoons vinegar
salt & pepper

Place all the ingredients in a large bowl and mix well. Refrigerate for
at least half and hour before serving.

Russian Salad

Serve 8 for starters / 4 for main course

225g / 8 oz potatoes, peeled, cooked and diced
1 carrot, peeled and diced
1 beetroot, skinned, cooked and diced
1 small cauliflower, trimmed, blanched and broken
1 medium turnip, peeled, cooked and diced
2 tomatoes, skinned and diced
150ml / 5 fl oz mayonnaise
1 tablespoon lemon juice
125g / 4 oz cooked peas
125g / 4 oz cooked prawns
4 cucumbers in brine, chopped
50g / 2oz capers
8 pitted black olives, halved
8 anchovies, sliced
salt & pepper

1. Thin the mayonnaise with the lemon juice and mix in all the ingredients.

2. Season well and make sure the olives, capers and anchovies are arranged above the other ingredients.

Waldorf Salad

Serves 4 as a side salad

500g / 1lb 2oz eating apples, peeled, cored, sliced and diced
½ freshly squeezed lemon juice
150ml / 5 fl oz mayonnaise
1 lettuce with flat leaves
½ head celery, trimmed and sliced
2oz / 50g walnut pieces, chopped
1 tablespoon sugar

1. Dip the apples in lemon juice, sugar and some mayonnaise at least 30 minutes before hand, in order to prevent discolouration.

2. Place the lettuce leaves in a salad bowl. Add the celery, remaining mayonnaise and walnuts to the diced apple mix and toss well.

3. Spoon onto the salad and decorate with sliced apples.

Dips

When it comes to dips, the Greeks, Turks and Persians become the real recipe makers. These days the majority of Europeans are adopting the eating habits of this part of the world where food is everything. You don't have to be hungry to have a dip of some sort. Dips are accompaniment to food and drink. In some countries, the waiters automatically bring a selection of dips while you are waiting for your main course.

Hummus

Serves 4

450g / 16oz / 2 cans cooked or 225g / 8oz dried chickpeas soaked over night and boiled until tender.
juice of 2 large lemons
70ml / 5 tablespoons olive oil
2 cloves garlic, crushed
150ml / 5 fl oz tahini
seasoning

1. Drain and place the peas in the blender. Gradually add the lemon juice while blending to bring it to a smooth texture.
2. Add the tahini paste, oil and garlic and blend again for a few seconds.
3. Season with salt and pepper.
4. Place in a dish, close the lid tightly and refrigerate.
5. When serving, decorate with some fresh parsley and serve with hot pita bread.

Mustard

Serves 4

3-4 tablespoons mayonnaise
4-6 tablespoons soured cream
2-3 tablespoons whole grain mustard
2-3 tablespoon finely chopped gherkins

Whisk the cream and mayonnaise, add the mustard and gherkins and blend again.
Season and place in a bowl and refrigerate for a few hours before serving.
This dip is best served with sausages or meatballs.

Yoghurt

Serves 4

600ml / 1 pint natural yoghurt
1 clove garlic, chopped finely
1 small red onion, finely chopped
30g / 1 oz fresh mint or basil, finely chopped
seasoning

Put all your ingredients in a large mixing bowl and whisk for a few seconds.
Place in a serving bowl and refrigerate a few hours before serving.
Serve with hot pita bread.

Blue Cheese

Serves 4

135ml / 4 fl oz soured cream
1 clove garlic, crushed
125g / 4oz blue stilton cheese, crumbled
juice of 1 lemon
seasoning

Place all the ingredients in a blender and blend into a smooth texture, season with salt and pepper.
Place in a bowl and decorate with chopped fresh tarragon or chives before serving.
Serve with crudités and French bread.

Hot and Spicy BBQ

Serves 4

225g / 8oz can tomatoes or 4 large fresh tomatoes, seeds discarded and chopped
3-4 fresh chillies, chopped
1 clove garlic, chopped
1 teaspoon Tabasco sauce
1 tablespoon soy sauce
1 small onion
salt & pepper

1. Place all the tomatoes, garlic and onion in the blender and blend until smooth.

2. Add salt and pepper and chillies with Tabasco and soy sauce and blend again.

3. Place in a fridge for an hour and then serve with fries or sausages.

Dressings

Sun Dried tomato

2 chopped chillies
1 teaspoon garlic paste
1 teaspoon cracked black pepper
juice of 1 lemon
2-3 tablespoons oil
35ml / 1 fl oz wine vinegar
125g / 4oz sun dried tomato paste
50g / 2 oz chopped sun dried tomatoes

Blend all the ingredients together, place in a suitable container and refrigerate.

Sun Dried Tomato Salsa

200g / 7oz tomato ends, chopped
25g / 1 oz coriander, chopped
100g / 3 ½ oz red onion, finely chopped
50g / 2oz sun dried tomato paste
20g / 1oz garlic paste
50g / 2 oz chopped sun dried tomatoes
seasoning

Blend all the ingredients together. Place in a suitable container and refrigerate.

Avocado Salsa

2 large red onions, finely diced
4 ripe avocados, peeled and diced
25g / 1oz coriander, finely chopped
500g / 1 lb 2 oz tomato ends
5g garlic paste / 1 teaspoon garlic, finely crushed
seasoning

Blend all the ingredients together. Place in a container and refrigerate.

French

90ml / 6 tablespoons oil
30ml / 2 tablespoons vinegar
30ml / 2 tablespoons lemon juice
1 egg yolk
15ml / 1 tablespoon whole grain / Dijon mustard
pinch cracked black pepper
seasoning

1.   Place all the ingredients in a bowl and whisk or shake until well
      blended

2.   Store in a screw topped jar or a bottle. Shake well before use as
      the oil will separate.

Mustard

1 tablespoon flour
pinch cayenne pepper
2 tablespoons sugar
1 tablespoon whole grain mustard or 1 teaspoon mustard powder
150ml / ½ pint milk
2 egg yolks, beaten
60 ml / 4 tablespoons cider vinegar

1. Mix all the ingredients except the egg and vinegar, with a little
    milk to a smooth texture.

2. Heat the remainder of milk and add to the mixture, bringing to
    the boil while stirring constantly.

3. Cool it down. Add the yolk and return to the heat to thicken, but
    do not allow it to boil.

4. Remove from the heat, allow to cool then add the vinegar and
    mix.

5. Store in a screw top jar.

Thousand Island

15ml / 1 tablespoon chopped stuffed olives
15ml / 1 tablespoon finely chopped onions
1 hard boiled egg, shelled and chopped
1 tablespoon chopped green pepper
1 tablespoon chopped fresh parsley
5ml / 1 teaspoon tomato purée

1. Mix all the ingredients together. Add 1 pint of olive oil and place in a screw top jar or bottle.

2. If you add this mixture to mayonnaise, you create a mayonnaise dressing.

Marinades

Peri peri

Chopped chillies
Garlic paste
Cracked black pepper
Lemon juice
Oil
Wine vinegar
Tomato paste

1. Blend all the ingredients together. Marinade your chicken pieces in the mixture for at least 24 hours in the fridge before frying or grilling.
2. The ingredient measures depends upon how much meat you are using and how strong you want the flavour. Taste depends on the chefs choice.

French

250g / 9oz French mustard
250g / 9oz oil
250g / 9 oz lemon juice
15g / ½ oz chilli powder
15g / ½ oz cumin
25g / 1 oz garlic paste

1. Blend all the ingredients together and store in a container. Cover and refrigerate.
2. This marinade is normally used for BBQ and lamb kebabs.

Hot & Spicy

4 chillies, finely chopped
1 clove garlic, crushed
135ml / 4 fl oz oil
1 tablespoon tomato paste
30g / 1 oz mint, dried
1 teaspoon dried chillies
juice of 1 lemon
salt & pepper

Place all the ingredients in a blender until mixed well. Transfer the mixture to a container. Cover and refrigerate.
This marinade can be used for either red meat or chicken.

Gooseberry Sauce

1 kg / 2lb 4oz tin gooseberries
1 kg / 2lb 4oz sugar
1 litre 800 ml / 3 pints water

1. Put the sugar and gooseberries with its juice and water in a pan and simmer until the gooseberries have broken down and the sauce is running red.
2. Chill the sauce. Place in a suitable container, cover and refrigerate.
3. You may use most fruits in order to make a sauce in this way.

Onion Marmalade

1 kg / 2lb 4 oz red onion, peeled, cut in half and finely sliced
1 litre / 35 fl oz orange juice
250g / 9oz sugar

1. Place all the ingredients in a pan and simmer until the juice has reduced to a thick consistency.
2. Remove from the heat. Cool the mixture and transfer to a container, cover and refrigerate.

Orange Marmalade

8 oranges
1kg / 2 lb 4 oz sugar
1 cinnamon stick
600ml / 1 pint water
1 litre / 35 fl oz orange juice

1. Peel all the oranges and with a sharp knife, turn them into julienne.
2. Place all the orange hearts into a blender and blend until smooth.
3. Place this and all the other ingredients into a large pan and simmer until the fruit is reduced to a thick consistency.
4. Remove, cool and place in a container. Refrigerate.

Tip: Do not have any fear in trying something different but make sure you adopt the same procedure at all times. For instance, lemon marmalade is cooked in the same way but using lemon peel.

Accompaniments

Croutons

Bread cut offs
Cracked black pepper
Oil
Grated Parmesan cheese

1. Cut the bread into approximately one-inch lengths and place in an oven tray.
2. Drizzle the oil over the bread and sprinkle the cracked black pepper and Parmesan cheese over. Toss to cover all the bread pieces.
3. Place in the oven or under a grill making sure the bread is turned during toasting, until golden brown.
4. Cool down and place in a container. Do not cover as it would make them rubbery.
5. When serving soup, you can use these croutons instead of more conventional fried cubed sliced bread.

Melba Toast

1. Get some white thick or medium sliced bread.
2. Toast both sides of the bread. Cut off the crusty edge on all sides.
3. Place one hand over the bread to hold it down but do not press hard and with the other hand, use a bread knife to cut across the middle of the bread.
4. Toast the other side and place in a container. Do not cover or else it will go rubbery.
5. This could be served on its own with butter or with galantines and terrines.

97

Finger toast

Toast both sides of some medium or thin sliced bread under the grill. Cut off the crusty edges. Cut the bread into fingers and place in a container. Finger toast is normally served with pâté.

Buttered Brown Bread

Use medium brown bread or granary bread and slice as required. Butter on one side of each slice. Take two slices and stick them together, cut off the edges. Place a cup or cutter over the bread and press hard to cut through. Bang the cup on the bread board to loosen the bread shape. This is normally served with prawn cocktail or any dressed starter.

Dumplings

100g / 4oz self raising flour
50g / 2oz shredded suet
pinch salt & pepper

Mix the flour, suet, salt and pepper in a bowl with sufficient water to make an elastic dough. Divide into about 16 portions and with lightly floured hands, turn them into small balls. You may either grill them or add them to soup, simmering for 15 minutes.

Zatsiki

250g / 9oz yoghurt
½ of a cucumber, chopped and finely diced
1 clove garlic, finely diced
1 pinch each of dried mint and dried basil
salt & pepper

Add the ingredients to the yoghurt and mix well.
Refrigerate for 30 minutes before serving.

Light recipes

Cous Cous

3 sachets cous cous
50g / 2oz onion
50g / 2oz mixed peppers
50ml / 2 fl oz vinaigrette
75g / 3 oz finely chopped tomato ends

1.   Boil three pints of water and a little salt. Remove from the heat
     and dunk the cous cous sachets in the hot water for exactly one
     minute.

2.   Open the sachets and turn out onto a tray, break up the lumps
     with a fork and quickly cool.

3.   Finely chop the peppers, tomato and onion and mix into the cous
     cous. Add the vinaigrette and season well with salt and pepper.

4.   Place in a suitable container. Cover and refrigerate.

Caponata

500g / 1 lb 2 oz aubergine
200g / 7oz tomatoes
200g / 7oz celery
200g / 7oz onion
100g / 3 ½ oz olives
50ml / 2 fl oz oil
20g / 1 oz dried basil
30g / 1 ½ oz garlic paste

1. Cut the olives in half and the rest of the vegetables into cubes.
    Mix well in a large bowl.

2. Add the oil and garlic paste. Add basil and season well, mix
    again.

3. Transfer into a roasting dish and place in the oven for about 20
    minutes or until the vegetables are softened.

4. Remove from the oven, cool and put into a suitable container.
    Cover and refrigerate.

Rata-toie

500g / 1 lb 2 oz aubergines
500g / 1 lb 2 oz courgettes
250g / 9 oz onion
1 bunch celery
2 heads of leeks
250g / 9 oz mixed peppers
1 clove garlic
1 kg / 2 lb 4 oz chopped tomatoes
4 bay leaves
135ml / 4 fl oz oil
pinch oregano
salt & pepper

1.	Slice the vegetables in thick chunky pieces and place in a roasting pan.

2.	Add oil, tomatoes, bay leaves, garlic, oregano, salt and pepper and mix well.

3.	Place the pan in the oven until the vegetables are softened and browned (about 20-30 minutes).

4.	Remove, cool, place in a container and refrigerate.

Copidyka

Serves 8

900g / 2lb minced lamb
1 large onion, finely diced
50g / 2 oz fresh ginger, grated or finely chopped
1 clove garlic, crushed
200g / 7 oz fresh coriander, finely chopped
1 teaspoon turmeric powder
salt & pepper

1. Place all the ingredients in a large bowl and mix well. Place the bowl in the fridge for 2 hours.

2. Use your finger to mould it in to shape around a skewer. You may need to wet your hand with water to avoid meat sticking to them.

3. Spread a sheet of cling film on a board and place the copidyka in the centre and roll the cling film round the meat. You should be able to make 8 of these.

4. Place on a tray in the fridge for another 2 hours, remove cling film before cooking on the grill or BBQ.

5. Serve with flour tortilla or pita bread and mixed salad. Place the copidykers on top of the salad and drizzle some zatsiki (see recipe on page 98) on top. Alternatively, serve it with rice.

Mushroom & Spinach Pancake

2 pancakes
100g / 3 ½ oz sliced field mushrooms
50g / 2 oz fresh or baby spinach
30g / knob of butter
10g / ½ oz tarragon
pinch cracked black pepper
salt & pepper

1. Place the butter in a frying pan and sauté the mushrooms, tarragon and spinach. Season well.

2. Warm the pancakes in the microwave or under the grill.

3. Place the contents in the centre of the pancake and roll to form a sausage shape.

4. Serve with fresh crisp salad and new potatoes.

Wexford Peppered Mushrooms

Serves 2

2 thick slices of bread
150g / 5 oz closed cob mushrooms
2 tablespoon finely chopped onion
salt & pepper
2 teaspoons cracked black pepper
knob of butter
135ml / 4 fl oz cream
135ml / 4 fl oz brown sauce

1. Deep or pan fry the bread and cut in half to make a triangle. Place in the centre of the plate so that the points of the triangle touch each other.

2. Place the butter in a pan with the onion and mushroom over a high heat, toss and turn for 2 minutes. Season well.

3. Add the cracked pepper and toss. Add the brown sauce and cream and let it simmer to reduce.

4. Place the mushrooms over the fried bread and drizzle the sauce over. It is best served with a salad garnish.

Mushrooms a'la Grecque

Serves 4

2 tablespoons olive oil
1 large onion, finely chopped
1 clove garlic, crushed
2 tablespoons tomato purée
2 glasses / 270 ml / 9 fl oz red wine
1 tablespoon coriander seeds, crushed
500g / 1 lb 2 oz button mushrooms
1 teaspoon sugar
225g / 8 oz fresh tomatoes, seeded and chopped / 8oz tinned tomatoes, chopped
bouquet garni
seasoning including dry and chopped fresh coriander

1. Heat the oil in a frying pan. Add the garlic and onion and cook for 4-5 minutes.

2. Stir in the tomato purée and wine, bouquet garni, coriander seeds and sugar. Add seasoning, mushrooms and tomatoes and cook gently for about 10 minutes on a low heat.

3. Remove the bouquet garni and spoon out the mushrooms and the sauce onto a plate.

4. This is normally served with rice or fries.

Chicken Frittata

3 eggs
25-30g / 1 oz baby spinach
½ sliced cooked chicken breast
25g / 1 oz pine nuts
25g / 1 oz mache lettuce

1. Beat the eggs in a large bowl. Add seasoning.
2. Mix the pine nuts, spinach, mache and chicken.
3. Put the mixture in a hot oiled frying pan and cook on a low heat. Finish cooking the top under the salamander or grill.
4. Transfer the frittata upside down on to the plate. It is best served with salad garnish and fries.

Smoked Salmon avocado salsa brush

Serves 2

2 ciabatto bread sliced in half length ways
100g / 3 ½ oz avocado salsa (refer to recipe page 91)
100g / 3 ½ oz sliced smoked salmon
25g / 1 oz garlic olive oil

1. Spread the fluffy side of the bread with garlic oil or garlic butter and toast under the grill.
2. Put a blob of avocado salsa on the middle of each piece and sprinkle the slices of salmon over the top.
3. Return to the grill until the salmon is warmed. Serve on a plate with salad garnish.

Brie Salsa Panini

Serves 2

2 panini bread sliced in half lengthways
100g / 3 ½ oz avocado salsa
150g / 5 oz brie slices

1. Place the brie slices on the bottom half, spread the avocado salsa on the top half. Put the halves together.

2. Either cook the panini under a char grill or on the silex to give a pattern before serving.

3. It is best served with salad garnish and fries.

Garlic Bread

You may use any bread for garlic bread. For the garlic butter, place 250g butter, 250g margarine, 2 tablespoons of garlic powder or 2 crushed fresh garlic clove and 50g dried parsley. Place all the ingredients in a blender and mix until smooth. Place in a container. Cover and refrigerate.

Knowing your fish

Fish is wonderful. It is healthy and is low in fat and carbohydrates. Fish has vitamins A and D, is a rich source of protein and can easily be digested. Have you ever fallen in love with a fish? I did when I was seven years old and that is why I have a passion for fish cookery.
Not all fish are freshly available all the year round. Most are available frozen which is cheaper and will hold the flavour.

Shell fish: such as Clams, Crabs, Cray fish, Lobster, Mussels, Prawns, Oysters and Scampi (Dublin Bay prawns).
Fresh water fish: Salmon, Trout, Perch, Pike, Roach, Tench, Carp, Eels, Grayling and fresh water Bream.
Sea fish: Deep sea water: Also known as white or Demersal fish: Anchovies, Sea bass, Sea bream, Brills, Escalor, Haddock, Halibut, John Dory, Monk fish, Mullet (red or grey), Octopus, Plaice, Sardine, Skate, Smelt, Sole (lemon or Dover), Squid, Sturgeon, Tuna, Turbot.
Surface sea water: Also known as oily or pelagic fish, such as: Kippers, Sprats, Bloaters, Pilchards, Herrings, Whitebait.
My favourites are King Prawns, Marlin, Sword fish, Red Snapper and Scottish Salmon. I have tried to give you easy to follow recipes for most of the above and for fish related sauces refer to page 23.

Fish sauces

Some of the most popular fish recipes are dependant upon interesting sauces and garnishes. Listed below are a number of appropriate sauces for fish with the easy cooking methods on pages 23 - 27.

Mustard	A'l'Ail
Tartare	Rouille
Normandy	Tarragon
Diplomat	Minute
Admiral	Raifort
Oyster	Watercress
Lyonnaise	Hawaiian
Cucumber	Anchovy and capers
Bearnaise	Citrus fruits
White mushroom	Meuniere
Mornay	Florentine
Epicure	Rochelaise
Lobster	Veronique
Espagnole	Lemon
Epinard	Puttanesca

Monkfish Terriaki on Grilled Apple

Pan fried Monkfish in apple and shoya sauce nestled on a bed of green apples

175g – 225g / 6-8oz Monkfish
60ml / 2 ½ fl oz shoya or soy sauce
1 teaspoon white sugar
60ml / 2 ½ fl oz apple juice
60ml / 2 ½ fl oz white wine
knob butter / 2 tablespoons olive oil

1. Pan fry the monkfish in a little butter, add the shoya or soy sauce and sugar and stir.

2. Add the apple juice and wine, simmer until reduced.

3. Grill 5 slices of apple and put on a plate.

4. Place the monkfish on top of the apple and pour the sauce over.

Persian Golf Escalor

Pan fried Escalor with turmeric and mustard cream

1 escalor
½ chopped onion
1 teaspoon turmeric
1 teaspoon English mustard
60ml / 2 ½ fl oz fish stock
60ml / 2 ½ fl oz cream
60ml / 2 ½ fl oz béchamel
30ml / 2 teaspoons olive oil

1. Put the escalor together with chopped onion in the frying pan.
    Add 2 teaspoons olive oil and fry for 2-3 minutes on each side.

2. Stir the onion thoroughly, add turmeric and mustard. Stir and add
    the fish stock, béchamel and cream, simmer and season to taste.

3. Reduce the sauce and drizzle on the plate. Place the escalor on
    top.

Brill Vieux Carre Papillote

Brill fillet with mixed peppers, prawns and spring onion in an envelope

1 Brill fillet 150-225g / 6-8oz
1 tablespoon olive oil
¼ green pepper, chopped
¼ red pepper, chopped
1 spring onion, chopped
1 teaspoon chopped thyme, oregano and tarragon mix
1 large fresh tomato
juice of 1 lemon
25g / 1oz Dublin Bay prawns

1. Make an envelope using a double thickness of foil. Grease the inside with olive oil.

2. Fry the chopped peppers, spring onions and herbs in a pan, add the chopped tomato and cook until tender. Then add the lemon juice.

3. Put the Brill fillet in the envelope and place the prawns on top. Add the seasoning and pour the juice over. Fold the foil, leaving an air space.

4. Bake in the oven for about ten minutes. The envelope should be opened in front of the diners.

Halibut Montecarlo

Halibut steak with Dill and Mustard cream

150-225g / 6-8 oz Halibut steak
1 teaspoon Dijon mustard
¼ onion, chopped
200ml / 7 fl oz béchamel
50ml / 2 fl oz cream
sprinkle fresh or 1 teaspoon dried dill
60ml / 2 ½ fl oz white wine
knob butter

1. Pan fry the butter with the chopped onion and Dijon mustard.

2. Add béchamel, white wine, cream and the dill

3. Simmer and reduce. Season to taste.

4. Pour the sauce in the middle of the plate and place the cooked halibut on top.

Supreme of Salmon Veronic with Crispy Leek Julienne

Poached Salmon fillet, grape sauce with Crispy Leek

1 salmon fillet
50g / 2oz butter
1 small onion
50g / 2oz green seedless grapes
60ml / 2 ½ fl oz white wine
60ml / 2 ½ fl oz fish stock
¼ leek stalk
2 tablespoons vegetable oil
60ml / 2 ½ fl oz whipping cream

1.   Poach the salmon until tender. Melt the butter in the frying pan, add onion and fry for a minute.

2.   Add seedless grapes, fish stock, cream, wine and simmer to reduce.

3.   Deep fry the julienne of leek in the vegetable oil until crispy.

4.   Place the salmon in the centre of the plate, pour the grape sauce over and add the crispy leek to the top.

5.   Serve with potatoes and vegetables.

Turbot Greens with Red Wine Dressing

Grilled turbot on stir fry greens, with horseradish dumpling and red wine dressing.

300g Turbot
1 tablespoon horseradish (relish)
100g / 3 ½ oz ready made dumpling mix (see page 98)
150ml / 5 fl oz fish stock
150g / 5oz greens (celery, leek, mange tout)
25g / 1oz butter
2 tablespoons red wine dressing (red wine added to brown sauce)
30 ml / 2 ½ fl oz olive oil

1. Dust the turbot, brush over with butter and grill until tender.

2. Pan fry the julienne of greens with a little olive oil. Add the grated horseradish to dumpling mix before poaching it.

3. Sit the greens in the centre of the plate with the turbot and a dumpling on top. Spoon the red wine dressing round the outside.

Samaki Wanazi

Zanzibar Bream African Curry and Rice

175 – 225g / 6-8oz Bream
50g / 2oz chopped onion
½ clove garlic, chopped
1 teaspoon curry powder
1 fresh chilli, chopped
50ml / 2 fl oz olive oil
1 teaspoon tomato puree
juice of 1 lemon
1 small tub of natural yoghurt

1. Bone the fish and cut into 7-8 pieces. Heat the oil in the pan and fry the fish gently.

2. Add the onions, garlic, chilli and curry powder. Season generously.

3. Add the yoghurt and tomato puree along with the lemon juice, simmer to reduce.

4. Put a packet of basmati rice in a bowl and cook in the microwave for 1 ½ minutes.

5. Serve the rice upside down like a mountain on the side of the plate and the fish curry beside it.

Ginger Baked King Fish Caribbean Style

Heavily flavoured with ginger, King fish, West Indian style

125g / 6-8 oz King fish cutlet
1 teaspoon vegetable oil / olive oil
12 ½ g / ½ oz crushed ginger
¼ mixed peppers, chopped
¼ clove garlic, chopped
1 spring onion, chopped
60ml / 2 ½ fl oz pineapple juice
1 teaspoon corn flour / plain flour
1 teaspoon soy sauce
1 teaspoon paprika, salt & pepper mixed

1. Mix the herbs and seasoning with the corn or plain flour and coat the King fish with the mix.

2. Shallow fry the fish in a frying pan with the oil for 5-7 minutes together with chopped mixed peppers, ginger and garlic.

3. Add the pineapple juice and soy sauce and simmer to reduce.

4. Place the fish on a plate and pour the sauce over before serving.

Monk Fish Thermidor

Monk fish fillet with onion and mushroom in brandy cream

175 – 225g / 6-8oz Monkfish fillet
50g / 2oz chopped mushrooms
50g / 2oz chopped onions
200ml / 7fl oz béchamel
10g / 1/3 oz whole grain mustard
12 ½ ml / 1oz brandy
knob butter
35ml / fl oz cream

1.   Pan fry the monkfish in a little butter and dill. Add the onion and mushrooms.

2.   Add the brandy and flambé it. Add the béchamel and cream. Then add the wholegrain mustard, simmer to reduce and season to taste.

3.   Serve immediately on a plate and pour the juice over to finish.

Escovitch Almond Trout

Marinated Grilled Trout with almond and lemon butter

1 Trout (rainbow or fillet)
knob butter
60ml / 2 ½ fl oz wine vinegar
juice of 1 lemon
25g / 1oz almonds

1. Dust the trout with flour and place in the pan.

2. Pour the wine vinegar and the lemon juice over it.

3. Crush the almonds and mix with the butter. Spread over the fillet
    and bake under the grill for a few minutes until tender.

Admiral John Dory

Baked John Dory in a sauce of capers and anchovy cream

1 John Dory
knob of butter
10 capers
25g / 1oz anchovy fillets
juice of ½ lemon
150ml / 5 fl oz béchamel
60ml / 2 ½ fl oz cream

1.   Brush the John Dory with melted butter. Bake in the oven, skin side up, until tender.

2.   Pour the béchamel, cream and the lemon juice in a bowl and mix well.

3.   Place the remaining butter in a frying pan with the chopped capers and anchovies over a low heat. Add the cream mixture to the frying pan and simmer to reduce.

4.   Pour the sauce on the plate and place the John Dory in the middle.

Baked Citrus Lemon Sole

Baked citrus lemon sole with minted butter sauce

Lemon Sole
1 orange
1 lemon
50g / 2oz butter
10g / 1/3 oz fresh mint
1 glass / 150ml wine
2 tablespoons fish stock (see recipe)
1 teaspoon sugar

1.   Peel and dice one orange and lemon. Set aside.

2.   Put the lemon sole on an oven tray, which has been coated with
      butter. Brush the lemon sole with butter, make diamond shape
      patterns with the sharp end of a knife on the sole. Put the diced
      orange and lemon on top of the sole, pour a glass of wine over
      and bake in a preheated oven for 10 minutes.

3.   Melt the remaining butter in a frying pan with chopped mint and
      fish stock. Add the sugar and season well, simmer to reduce the
      sauce.

4.   Put the lemon sole in the centre of an oval plate. Pour the sauce
      over and garnish with a wedge of lemon. Serve with vegetables
      and potatoes.

Sword Fish Pacific Ocean

Swordfish, julienne of smoked salmon and watercress sauce

225g / 8oz swordfish steak
25g / 1oz smoked salmon julienne
15g / ½ oz chopped watercress
2 tablespoons fish stock (see recipe)
60ml / 2 ½ fl oz béchamel
60ml / 2 ½ fl oz whipping cream
1 glass of wine
knob of butter

1.   Pan fry the swordfish with a little butter. Add the smoked salmon, béchamel, chopped watercress and fish stock.

2.   Add wine and cream. Season to taste and simmer to reduce the sauce.

3.   Place the sauce in the middle of an oval plate and put the swordfish in the centre.

Baked Scallops Provencale

Baked scallops with Provencale sauce and julienne of vegetables

5 scallops
60ml / 2 ½ fl oz olive oil
1 teaspoon chopped garlic
225g / ½ lb chopped fresh tomatoes
1/3 pack chopped fresh basil
1 handful chopped fresh parsley
150g / 5oz julienne of vegetables

1. Pan fry the scallops with a little olive oil and garlic.

2. For the julienne use 1 small carrot, ½ small turnip and 1 stalk of
    celery. Add the vegetables and chopped tomato. Stir for 2-3
    minutes then add the chopped parsley and basil.

3. Simmer for one minute and serve.

Craft Cod with Prawn Gravy

Roast Cod with horseradish, Yorkshire pudding and prawn gravy

1 cod fillet
knob butter
shrimps (prawns)
150ml / 5 fl oz gravy granules and fish stock
2 teaspoons horseradish cream
2 teaspoons vegetable oil
Batter: 225g / 8oz plain flour
       3 eggs
       300ml / 10 fl oz milk

1. Brush the cod with melted butter and place on a buttered oven tray in the oven for 5-7 minutes.

2. Make the batter for the Yorkshire pudding with horseradish cream. Oil the moulds and leave in the oven until smoking. Pour the batter (see recipe) inside the mould and bake in the oven until golden brown.

3. For the gravy, use the fish stock and gravy granules. Add the prawns and bring to the boil.

4. Place the cod in the centre of the plate. Pour the prawn gravy over and serve with Yorkshire pudding, vegetables and roast potatoes.

Dover Sole Normandy

Baked Dover sole with butter lemon sauce

1 Dover sole
knob butter
150 ml / 5 fl oz fish stock
1 egg yolk
juice of 1 lemon
2 tablespoons flour
60ml / 2 ½ fl oz white wine

1. Dust the Dover sole with flour. Put in a greased oven tray and
    brush the sole with butter. Leave in the oven until golden.

2. Melt a little butter in a frying pan for the sauce, add flour and stir
    until brown. Add fish stock and lemon juice. Add the egg yolk
    and then stir thoroughly.

3. Add the wine and bring to the boil to reduce the consistency.

4. Place the Dover sole in the centre of an oval plate, pour the sauce
    over and place a lemon twist on top.

Tuna Puttanesca Vera Cruz

Tuna steak on fried bread and Mexican sauce

200-225g / 7-8 oz tuna steak
1 teaspoon garlic
knob butter or 2 teaspoons olive oil
25g / 1oz anchovies
6 capers
4 olives
2 chopped fresh tomatoes
60ml / 2 ½ fl oz fish stock
1 slice of bread

1. Pan fry the tuna with a little butter for 2-3 minutes on each side together with crushed garlic and chopped olives, capers and tomatoes.

2. Add a little water and fish stock, then the anchovies. Season to taste and simmer to reduce the sauce.

3. Cut the edges of the bread, fry and put in the centre of the plate.

4. To serve, sit the tuna steak on the fried bread and pour the sauce on top.

Swordfish with Sauce Anchovy Cream

Fried Swordfish with Anchovy cream, noodles, crispy Parma ham and coriander

Swordfish
Knob of butter
75g / 3oz fresh or dried noodles
1 slice Parma ham
¼ onion
1/8 leek
1 clove crushed garlic
50ml / 2 fl oz white wine
50ml / 2 fl oz fish stock
dairy whipping cream
25g / 1oz anchovy fillets
1 handful of coriander

1. Dust the fish with flour and pan fry both sides on a low heat until tender.
2. Melt the butter in a separate frying pan. Add the chopped onions and garlic and leeks and toss until tender. Add chopped anchovy fillets and fry for a further minute.
3. Add the wine, fish stock, cream and simmer to reduce.
4. In a separate frying pan, fry the coriander and diced or shredded Parma ham. Cook the noodles in boiling water for 2-3 minutes. Put the noodles in the centre of the plate, the swordfish on top and cover with sauce and crown with fried Parma.

Knowing your meat

When training my students, the first question I am always asked is why do we bake this and fry that and boil the other part of the meat? So lets get to know what we are buying from our butcher and lets make sure we get the right meat for the right dish. Good cooking is the combination of the right quality of meat and a good sauce. So here is an explanation of the various cuts of meat and the best way of cooking them.

Pork

Pork is relatively cheap because of its popularity in the western world. Pork has different cuts and uses.

LEG OF PORK: is known as chump end. It is basically used for roasting

GAMMON: According to their different cuts are known as corner, hock and middle and can all be used for boiling, grilling and baking.

BACON: is the thin slices of belly and can be fried, grilled or stewed. There are different kinds of bacon known for their quality and taste such as:

1. Streaky bacon   2. Rindless back bacon   3. Smoked bacon

PRIME JOINTS: Leg and fillet

PRIME CUTS: Pork loin and pork chops

MEDIUM CUTS: Spring and spare ribs which can be used for roasting, boiling and stewing.

Poultry

Poultry are known as chicken, duckling, turkey, goose and guinea fowl. Chicken is the cheapest of these meats and widely available. Due to its versatility, chefs and cooks can create a selection of dishes, as all its cuts are useable:

1. Chicken supreme is the breast with part of the wing. It is usually used for frying, grilling and B.B.Q.
2. Chicken fillet is also known as chicken breast but with no bone. It is used for frying, boiling, B.B.Q. and grilling.
3. Chicken legs are used for frying, casserole and grilling
4. Chicken wings are usually used for frying and B.B.Q.

Beef

Beef is divided into three different cuts:

Prime cuts are tender and have extremely good flavour. Prime cuts are good for frying and grilling such as: 1. Sirloin steak   2. Fillet steak

Medium cuts are used for roasting or slow cooking in the oven, such as:
                    1. Top side
                    2. Spare ribs

Course cuts are in need of very slow cooking. They can also be roasted in a low heat in the oven or boiled, such as:
                    1. Silver side
                    2. Shoulder or mutton
                    3. Neck or clod
                    4. Leg (hind) or Shin (fore)

Lamb

Lamb also has different cuts.   All lamb parts and cuts are used to create a great dinner.   In some Middle Eastern countries, the brains, tongue, hands and feet are also used to make a good stew as an appetizer or breakfast.

For roasting: leg of lamb, lamb shoulder, best end of neck and lamb loin are used.

For frying and B.B.Q: Lamb chops, lamb cutlets and lamb fillets from the top of the leg are used.

For stewing and casserole: Breast, neck and leg are best.

In this section I introduce you to more elaborate cookery. In compiling these recipes it has been assumed that the reader is familiar with the basics and has followed the book right from the start. This section contains recipes, all of which have been tested and served in restaurants all over the world. These recipes were primarily intended for teaching purposes. I hope that it will at the same time prove to be helpful to many people who are not involved in the catering profession.

Veal

Cotelettes De Veau a la Colbert
(Veal cutlets in Colbert style)

500g / 18oz fillet of veal, cut into neat thin pieces
2 tablespoons finely chopped onion
1 knob of butter
½ tablespoon oil
300ml / ½ pint Madeira sauce (see recipe)
1 teaspoon chopped parsley
2 large potatoes for Parisian and creamy potatoes (see recipe)
2 slices of bread cut in fancy shapes and fried
Seasoning

1. Place the butter and the oil in a frying pan. Add onion and fry lightly.
2. Add the veal pieces one by one and fry on both sides. Pour off any surplus fat.
3. Add the Madeira sauce and simmer gently for 2 minutes till the cutlets are tender and the sauce is reduced.
4. Add the parsley and simmer for a further minute.

To serve:
Arrange creamy potatoes round the plate. Place the Parisian potatoes in the centre of the plate. Place half of the cutlets on top of the Parisian potatoes and pour the sauce over the cutlets. To garnish, place fancy fried bread on top.

Paupiettes de veau
(Paupiettes of veal)

500g / 1lb 2 oz fillet of veal forcemeat
100g / 3 ½ oz bacon
Meat glaze
200g / 7 oz spinach puree
200g / 7 oz demi-glace (see recipe page 19)
400g / 14oz mash potato

1. Cut the veal into slices. Spread the forcemeat onto the veal and roll up.

2. Tie a slice of bacon round each roll. Braise the paupiettes. When ready, drain then remove bacon and trim.

3. Place the creamed mash in the centre of a round plate. Put the paupiettes round it in an up right position.

4. Pile up spinach puree on top of the mash in the middle.

5. Reduce the stock from the braising pot to a glaze. Add it to the demi-glace then pour the sauce round.

Blanquette de Veau

White Stew of Veal

500g / 1 lb 2 oz fillet of veal trim and cut into neat pieces
1 large onion, finely diced
25g / 1 oz bouquet garni
Knob of butter
25g 1 oz flour
6 button mushrooms, finely sliced
1 tablespoon cream
1 egg yolk
1 tablespoon lemon juice
Seasoning

1. Place the veal in a pan and cover with water. Add half of the diced onion to the pan and season with salt, pepper and bouquet garni. Bring to boil until tender and skim.

2. For the sauce, place the butter and lemon juice with the rest of the onion and mushrooms and shallow fry. Add flour, add the stock from the meat (after straining). Mix the cream and egg yolk together. Add to the sauce and reduce.

3. Place the veal in the centre of a round plate and pour the sauce over it.

Involtini a'lla Milanese

(baked breaded escalope of veal)

175 g / 6 oz veal escalope, battened (flattened with a rolling pin)
2 tablespoons tomato sauce (see recipe)
50g / 2 oz cheddar grated or Swiss cheese
50g / 2 oz breadcrumbs
1 egg, beaten
135 ml / 1 cup of milk
2 tablespoons flour
1 tablespoon oil
Pinch freshly chopped parsley

1. Place the flour in a large bowl. Place the breadcrumbs in a separate large bowl.   Place the egg mixture in a large bowl.
2. Chop the parsley leaves finely and place on a plate.
3. Coat the veal with flour. Add the egg mixture and cover the escalope. Place the escalope into the breadcrumbs and cover thoroughly. Press and shape the escalope with the palm of your hand.
4. Heat the oil in a large frying pan. Place the escalope into the pan and shallow fry on both sides until golden brown.
5. Place the escalope in an oven dish, spread the tomato sauce over the top and place the cheese on top of the tomato. Place in a preheated oven for five minutes until the cheese is completely melted. Remove from the oven and serve immediately, sprinkled with the parsley.

Saltimbocca al la Romana

Escalope of veal

Serves 4

In Italian Saltimbocca means 'jump in the mouth'. In English it is known as Escalope of veal.

500g / 1 lb 2 oz / 8 thin slices of veal
125g / 4 oz butter
25g / 1 oz sage dried or 50g / 2 oz freshly chopped
8 slices of Parma ham (Prosciutto)
135 ml / 4 fl oz white wine
1 clove garlic, crushed
135 ml / 4 fl oz cream
80g / 3 oz cheddar
2 tablespoons finely chopped onion

1. Place a slice of Parma ham in the middle of the thin slice of veal (use a rolling pin to flatten the veal). Put the shredded cheese in the centre of the meat and roll. Use a wooden skewer to hold together.
2. Place the butter with garlic and onion in a large frying pan on a low heat, fry the veal rolls until sealed completely. Add the wine and cream.
3. Simmer to reduce. Meanwhile add sage and seasoning.
4. Put two in the centre of the plate and drizzle the sauce around them.

Involtini al la Mafioza

Veal escalope and capers with tomato dressing

Serves 4

12 thin escalops of veal
1 clove garlic, crushed
2 tablespoons olive oil
225g / 8 oz / 1 can chopped tomato
135 ml / 4 fl oz white wine
50g / 2 oz capers
50g / 2 oz pitted black olives
25g / 1 oz thyme

1.   Pan fry the veal individually and keep on a separate plate. Fry the garlic in the same pan, season and add the wine.

2.   Add tomato, capers and olives. Return the veal to the frying pan and simmer to reduce the sauce.

3.   To serve, place three escallops in the centre of the plate and spoon the sauce to cover them. Garnish with fresh thyme.

Beef

Bistecca a'lla pizaiola
(Sirloin steak in a sauce of pizaiola)

225g / 8 oz sirloin steak
1 tablespoon oil
1 clove garlic, crushed
2 anchovy fillets
15g / ½ oz capers
4 pitted black olives
125g / 4 oz seeded and finely diced fresh tomatoes / half can chopped tomatoes
135 ml / 4 fl oz white wine / 1 glass
Pinch oregano
Salt and pepper

1. Leave the fat on the edge of the steak and pan fry on both sides with garlic, anchovies, capers and olives.
2. Add wine and tomatoes. Add oregano and season well with salt and pepper.
3. Reduce sauce on a low heat and serve immediately.

To serve:
This is best served with some roasted potatoes and fresh vegetables.

Entrecote stilton
(Stilton steak)

225g / 8 oz sirloin of beef, fat free and brushed with oil
Knob of butter
1 tablespoon finely chopped onion
1 tablespoon béchamel
1 tablespoon cream
50g / 2 oz crushed Stilton cheese
35 ml / 1 ½ fl oz white wine

1. Pan fry the sirloin lightly to seal on both sides, then remove and place in an oven dish.

2. In a separate frying pan, place butter and onion and fry into golden. Add béchamel, cream and wine.

3. Simmer over a low heat until the sauce is reduced. Pour the sauce over the steak and cover it with stilton cheese. Place in pre heated oven for 5 minutes in order for the cheese to melt down.

N.B. Depending on how you want the steak to be cooked, make sure you drain off all the excess oil before adding the sauce.

Chateaubriand a' la béarnaise

Serves 2

500g / 1 lb 2 oz double fillet of beef
1 small onion, finely diced
50g / 2 oz fresh tarragon finely chopped or 1 teaspoon dried tarragon
Knob of butter
2 egg yolks
2 tablespoons Béchamel (see recipe)
1 tablespoon white wine vinegar
1 tablespoon cream
Pinch cracked black pepper
seasoning

1.   Place the butter in a frying pan. Add onion and tarragon. Toss
     and turn for one minute and then add wine vinegar and
     béchamel.

2.   Beat the egg yolk into the cream and add to the sauce. Add
     crushed black pepper and season to taste. Simmer to reduce
     sauce.

3.   For the fillet, wipe and trim the steak, brush over with little oil
     and grill, turning frequently until well browned but under done.

4.   Place the fillet on a dish and serve with the béarnaise sauce
     separately.

Filet de boeuf au poivre
(Pepper fillet)

1 x 225g / 8 oz fillet steak
Knob of butter
Half of small onion or 1 tablespoon finely chopped onion
1 tablespoon cracked black pepper
1 tablespoon demi-glace (see recipe page 19)
1 tablespoon cream
Splash brandy

1. Brush the fillet with oil then grill or fry on both sides to your preferred likeness.

2. For the pepper sauce, place the butter and onion in a frying pan and brown in a low heat. Add demi-glace and cream, season with black pepper and simmer to reduce.

3. Place the fillet on a plate and before pouring the sauce over, add a splash of brandy.

Filleto al la Bascaiola
(Fillet steak in bascaiola style)

1 225g / 8 oz fillet of beef
3 button mushrooms, sliced
1 tablespoon finely chopped onion
1 teaspoon French mustard
Knob of butter
1 tablespoon demi– glace (see recipe page 19)
1 tablespoon cream
35 ml / 1 ½ fl oz red wine
Seasoning

1. Brush the fillet with oil and pan fry or grill as you like.

2. Fry butter, mushrooms and onion. On a low heat toss and turn until brown.

3. Season with salt and pepper, add mustard and stir. Add red wine, demi glace and cream to the sauce and simmer to reduce.

4. Place the fillet on a plate and pour the sauce over it.

Filet de boeuf au paprika
(Fillet steak in a sauce of paprika)

1 225g / 8 oz fillet of beef
Knob of butter
1 tablespoon finely chopped onion
1 rasher of bacon, finely chopped
1 tablespoon cream
1 tablespoon demi glace (see recipe page 19)
1 teaspoon paprika
Splash of brandy
Seasoning

1.   Grill or pan fry the fillet to your taste. Place the butter in a frying
     pan, add onion and bacon then toss and turn until brown.

2.   Strain the fat, add paprika, demi-glace , cream and season well.
     Add brandy and simmer the sauce to reduce.

3.   Place the fillet on a plate and serve the sauce over it.

Tournedos Rossini

225g / 8 oz fillet steak, trimmed
1 croutons of bread, trimmed from the crusty edges into a round shape and fried
1 tablespoon pate
1 knob of butter
1 tablespoon finely diced onion
35 ml / 1 ½ fl oz dry sherry
1 tablespoon demi– glace (see recipe page 19)
1 teaspoon cracked black pepper

1. Pan fry or char grill the fillet to your liking. Place the butter in a frying pan with the onion over a low heat, season with black pepper and fry until golden.

2. Add sherry and demi– glace and simmer to reduce.

3. Place the bread in the centre of the plate. Place the fillet on top of the bread. Place the pate (could be bought from a supermarket) on top of the fillet. Pour the sauce over it.

Fillet tariyaki
(Fillet steak in Japanese style)

225g / 8 oz fillet, thinly sliced
Knob of butter
1 teaspoon garlic, crushed
1 teaspoon ginger, crushed
1 tablespoon soy sauce
1 glass / 135 ml / 4 ½ fl oz red wine
1 tablespoon demi– glace (see recipe page 19)

1. Pan fry or char grill the fillet slices. In a frying pan fry the garlic
    and ginger until golden, season well.

2. Add the soy sauce and the red wine and simmer for a minute on a
    low heat. Add demi– glace and simmer to reduce.

3. Place the fillet slices on a plate and pour the sauce over.

Filleto a'lla pepper Verdi
(Fillet steak with cream and green pepper corn)

225g / 8 oz fillet trimmed
Knob of butter
25g / 1 oz green peppercorn (dried) or pickled in vinegar from super markets
1 tablespoon finely chopped onion
1 tablespoon béchamel, (see recipe)
1 tablespoon cream
35 ml / 1 ½ fl oz white wine
Splash brandy
Seasoning

1.　Brush the fillet with oil and pan fry or char grill.

2.　Melt the butter in a frying pan with onion and green pepper corn over a low heat, toss and turn until brown. Season well with salt and pepper.

3.　Add white wine, cream and béchamel and simmer for two minutes until the sauce is reduced. Add brandy and pour over the fillet.

Du boeuf a' la bourguignon
(Fillet of beef bourguignon)

225g / 8 oz fillet of beef, trimmed and cut into medallions
1 tablespoon finely chopped onion
4-5 button mushrooms, quartered
1 knob of butter
½ teaspoon dried cinnamon
½ teaspoon dried paprika
½ teaspoon dried turmeric
1 tablespoon of demi– glace
135 ml / 1 glass red wine
Salt and pepper

1. Place the butter, beef and all the spices with the onion and mushrooms in a large frying pan and braise on a high heat for 2-3 minutes.

2. Add wine and demi– glace with very little water and simmer on a low heat until the sauce is reduced to a thick consistency.

3. This is usually served with French fries or rice.

Entrecote Diane
(Sirloin steak in Diane sauce)

225g / 8 oz sirloin steak trimmed neatly of fat, butterfly and battened
(cut in the middle and opened up, then flattened)
3 button mushrooms, finely diced
1 tablespoon finely diced onion
Knob of butter
1 tablespoon French mustard
1 tablespoon cream
Pinch cracked black pepper
1 tab spoonful demi– glace (see recipe)
35 ml / 1 ½ fl oz brandy
Seasoning

1. Spread the sirloin steak with mustard on both sides. Place the
    butter in a large frying pan, together with onion and mushrooms.

2. Place the steak in the pan and on top of the ingredients. Once the
    steak has changed colour, turn it over and add the cracked black
    pepper.

3. Add demi-glace, cream and seasoning and simmer until the sauce
    is reduced.

4. Splash the brandy over the sauce and serve immediately, placing
    the steak in the centre of a plate with the sauce over it.

Entrecote Forestiera
(Sirloin steak in forestiera style)

225g / 8 oz sirloin of beef, fat free and brushed with oil
Knob of butter
1 bacon rasher, finely diced
1 clove garlic, finely crushed
½ tablespoon finely diced onion
1 tablespoon finely diced mixed peppers
1 small potato, finely diced
1 tablespoon tomato sauce (see recipe)
135 ml / 4 ½ fl oz white wine
1 teaspoon dried basil

1.   Pan fry or grill the steak. Place the butter, onion, garlic, peppers, potato and bacon in the frying pan. Once all the ingredients have become tender, drain the excess fat.

2.   Add wine, tomato and a pinch of freshly chopped or dried basil.

3.   Simmer to reduce and serve immediately pouring the sauce over the steak.

Lamb

Cotlettes D'agneau en Persian
(lamb cutlets in Persian style)

250g / 9 oz minced lean lamb
270 ml / 9 fl oz / 2 glasses vegetable oil
1 large onion, grated
2 eggs, the yolk and white separated
1 teaspoon turmeric
200g / 7oz potato, boiled, peeled and mashed
1 clove garlic, crushed
Salt and pepper

1. Place the lamb, onion and garlic in a big bowl and mix well. Season with turmeric, salt and pepper. Add the yolk of egg to the mixture and mix again.
2. Pour the oil in a frying pan over a medium heat. Using the egg white, cover the palm of your hand and pick up a hand full of the mixture. Using your hand, shape into balls and press in order to get a firm texture. Slide the cutlet into the frying pan and fry until golden brown. Turn the cutlet to the other side and fry until golden brown.
3. Remove and place on a plate and cover with a kitchen towel to extract the excess oil from the cutlet. Repeat the same procedure for the rest of the meat.
4. Serve over mixed leaves with hot crusty bread.

Agneau a' la stincatto
(lamb shanks Greek style)

500g / 1 lb 2 oz / 2 lamb shanks
4 spoonfuls basil mash potatoes
2 fresh rosemary bunches / 1 tablespoon dried rosemary
135 ml / 4 ½ fl oz / one glass red wine
1 tablespoon crushed garlic
2 tablespoons demi-glace (see recipe page 19)
1 tablespoon finely chopped onion
Knob of butter
Seasoning

1.   Place the lamb in a large saucepan on medium heat and fill
     2/3rds with water.   Bring to the boil and simmer until the meat is
     tender - this is normally about an hour.

2.   Remove the lamb from the pan and put in an oven dish, cover
     with foil (shiny side down) and place in the oven.

3.   Place the butter and onion with garlic in a frying pan, stir for 2
     minutes over a low heat. Add the red wine, demi-glace and
     rosemary and simmer to reduce.

4.   Heat the mash potato in a microwave and place in the centre of
     the plate.

5.   Remove the lamb from the oven and place on top of the mash
     and pour the sauce over.

Cotlettes d'agneau a'la groseille
et romarin
(Lamb cutlets with red current and rosemary)

500g / 1 lb 2 oz best end neck of lamb, cut in half inch pieces
50g / 2 oz red currants fresh / frozen
1 tablespoon red current jelly
1 tablespoon demi-glace (see recipe)
1 teaspoon dried / 20g / 1 oz fresh rosemary
1 tablespoon finely chopped onion
Knob of butter
1 glass / 135 ml / 4 ½ fl oz red wine
Seasoning

1. Pan fry the cutlets with a little oil for 2 minutes on either side.
    Add onion and fry for a further 2 minutes, turning the cutlets
    around occasionally.

2. Season well and then add the wine and demi– glace and simmer
    for one minute.

3. Mean-while add the red currant jelly and red currants and
    rosemary, simmer until the sauce is reduced.

4. Place the lamb in the centre of a plate and cover with the sauce.

Kleftico
(spiced lamb knuckle on garlic mash)

500g / 1 lb 2 oz / 2 lamb knuckles
1 tablespoon oil
1 tablespoon finely chopped onion
200g / 7oz demi-glaze (see recipe page 19)
1 teaspoon thyme
50g / 2 oz freshly chopped coriander
20g / 1 oz fresh ginger, finely chopped
1 glass of red wine
2 tablespoons of demi-glace
1 teaspoon crushed black pepper
2 bay leaves
Salt and pepper
3 tablespoons of garlic mash potatoes

1.   Place the lamb in an oven dish. Add a little water, garlic, onion,
     herbs and spices with red wine and demi-glace. Cover the dish
     with foil. Place in the oven for approximately one and half hours
     at 220°C /425°F / Gas Mark 7.

2.   Heat the mash in the microwave and place in the centre of a
     plate. Remove the lamb from the dish and place in the centre of
     the mash and pour the sauce over it.

Lamb tikka masala
(potted lamb Indian style)

500g / 1 lb 2 oz lamb shoulder/ leg pieces neatly trimmed
1 clove garlic, crushed
1 onion, chopped
25g / 1 oz fresh ginger, finely chopped
1 teaspoon cumin
1 teaspoon turmeric
1 teaspoon dried chillies / 3 fresh chillies, finely sliced
1 teaspoon mustard seeds
25g / 1 oz finely chopped fresh mint
1 tablespoon coriander seeds
25g / 1 oz freshly chopped coriander
3 tablespoons yoghurt
2 tablespoons vegetable oil
3 fresh tomatoes, quartered
Salt and pepper

1. Place the lamb with oil in a saucepan. Add onion and braise for 5 minutes. Add all of the other ingredients. Cover with water and bring to the boil and simmer for an hour until the meat is tender.

2. Add water if necessary Reduce the sauce to a thick texture.

3. This is best served with rice, naan bread and popadom and some kind of chutney.

Qorme Sabzi
(Persian fresh herbs lamb casserole)

500g / 1 lb 2 oz lamb fillet/ lamb shanks, cut into one inch size pieces
with or without bones.
400 ml / 14 fl oz vegetable oil
1 large onion, finely diced
1 tablespoon turmeric
2 celery sticks, finely sliced
150g / 5 oz fresh spinach leaves, finely chopped
150g / 5 oz parsley, finely chopped
150g / 5 oz fresh dill, finely chopped
1 large leek (green onion leaves), finely sliced
3 dried limes
1 tablespoon tomato purée
1 tablespoon freshly squeezed lemon juice

1. Use half of the onion placing it in a sauce pan with lamb pieces
    and braise with a little oil for five minutes. Add turmeric, salt
    and pepper.

2. Add plenty of water to cover the meat. Add dried limes (making
    holes with a fork in order for water to get inside), bring to the
    boil and simmer for one hour.

3. In a large frying pan place all the vegetables and herbs and fry
    until almost black and reduced to a quarter. Remove and add the
    fried vegetables to the lamb and simmer for a further 5 minutes.

4. Stir in lemon juice and serve with plain rice.

Cotlettes D'Adneau En Chau-Froid
(Lamb cutlets in Chaud-froid style)

500g / 1 lb 2 oz best neck of lamb, chine bone removed
½ litre / 17 ½ fl oz béchamel sauce (see recipe)
135 ml / 4 ½ fl oz aspic jelly
1-2 spoonfuls cream
salt & pepper

1. Bind the lamb with string and wrap in greaseproof paper, place
    in a pan, cover with homemade stock or ready made stock and
    cook for half an hour to an hour.

2. Remove the lamb from the stock and cut. Divide into three
    quarter inch thickness.

3. For the sauce; heat the béchamel and add some liquid aspic jelly,
    season well. Wring through a Tammy cloth (muslin cloth) and
    add the cream and use when it has just begun to thicken.

4. Coat the lamb with Chaud-froid sauce and decorate with chopped
    aspic jelly. This is best served with salad.

NB: tomato sauce or brown sauce may be used instead of béchamel.
Colouring could also be used or you can mix the béchamel with
coloured pastes such as pea puree.

Agneau a'la Saint Germain
(Lamb cutlets saint germane style)

500g / 1 lb 2 oz best neck of lamb, chine bone removed and cut into ½ inch thickness
2 tablespoons oil
½ terrine foie-gras or potted chicken paste
½ litre chaud-froid sauce made with 1.2 béchamel and ½ green pea puree
135ml / 4 ½ fl oz aspic jelly
1-2 spoonfuls cream
1 egg white
sat & pepper
1 teaspoon colouring

1. Fry the lamb in a large frying pan, then press the farce with foie-gras on top of the cutlets.

2. Heat the béchamel in saucepan, add 200g pea puree paste and aspic jelly. Mix and pass through a sieve and tammy through the muslin, add the cream and the colouring.

3. When the mixture begins to thicken, coat the cutlets and decorate with the egg white and jelly pieces to crown over a bed of mixed leaves.

Chicken

Chicken, or pullet as the French call it, or polo according to the Italians, is so versatile that almost every part can be used in cooking. Chicken is the most economical and low fat source of protein. It is widely available and is an alternative to red meat. In this section, I will show you the various recipes and methods of cooking such as roasting, baking, frying, grilling, braising, stewing and casseroling.

There are many types of chickens such as:
1 – Boiler fryer chickens – weigh about 2 kilograms. They are inexpensive and perfect for making casseroles, grilling or frying.
2 – Roasting chickens – weigh more than 2 kilograms and have a higher fat content.
3 – Free-range chickens – have access to open areas and are fed a vegetarian diet that is also free from antibiotics and hormones. These chickens are meatier and more expensive than the massed produced ones and have more taste.
4 – Poussins (spatchcock) and Cornish hens – are so tiny that they will often serve only one person. Their meat is very tender and tasty.

Although chicken has come a long way from its beginning as a wild fowl in south east Asia, there are records of chicken being raised in China since 1400. Since the 1950's, chicken has become widely available as a result of the advent of mass production. For the same reason, the transmission of diseases has also escalated. Careful handling of raw poultry helps prevent this transmission. Chicken must be kept in a refrigerator for not more that 48 hours, or put in a freezer until it is needed. Chicken must be defrosted in the fridge for at least 24 hours before use. It should not be kept in room temperature for more than 2 hours and must be consumed within 2-3 days once it is cooked. Raw chickens can only be kept in the refrigerator for 2 days.

Chicken Kiev

Serves 1

200-225 g / 7-8 oz Chicken supreme
knob (50g/2oz) butter
1 teaspoon garlic clove, crushed
100g / 3 ½ oz white bread crumbs
1 large egg, beaten
50g / 2 oz flour
2 tablespoons oil
1 teaspoon Paprika
freshly chopped parsley

1. Open the breast of the chicken leaving the wing part intact and then beat the breast until flat.
2. Place the butter in the middle and cover it with garlic and paprika. Season with salt, pepper and crushed black pepper and seal it, ensuring that there is no gap.
3. Put the egg, flour and breadcrumbs in to separate bowls. Dip the chicken gently into flour, covering it completely and then into the egg mixture, making sure the whole breast is wet and sticky, then place it in the bread crumbs and roll it while holding it gently in your hand.
4. Place the chicken in a frying pan, with oil on a low heat and fry until golden brown all over.
5. To serve, place the chicken in the centre of a plate and cut open the top with a knife. Press down until some of the melted garlic butter comes out.
6. Garnish with freshly chopped parsley and serve with vegetables or a flavoured rice.

Chicken Milanese

Serves 1

150-175g / 5-6 oz chicken fillet
1 large egg, beaten
50g / 2 oz flour
100g / 3 ½ oz bread crumbs
3 tablespoons plum tomatoes, chopped
50g / 2 oz Cheddar cheese, grated
2 tablespoons oil
fresh coriander

1.   Beat the boned breast of chicken and dip it into flour, then dip
     into egg. Cover with breadcrumbs and place in a frying pan with
     some oil.

2.   Fry both sides in oil until golden brown then place in an
     ovenproof dish. Top it up with crushed tomato or sliced fresh
     tomato and crown it with your grated cheddar or Parmesan
     cheese. You may put it under the grill or in the oven for the
     cheese to be melted.

3.   To serve, place the chicken in the centre of the plate and garnish
     with fresh coriander. Serve with some freshly cooked vegetables.

Swiss Chicken

Serves 4

4 chicken breasts
8 slices Swiss cheese
5 tablespoons butter
2 tablespoons plain flour
½ cup chicken broth
½ cup milk
½ cup white wine
1 cup dry stuffing

1. Put the chicken in a baking dish and cover each one with 2 slices of Swiss cheese. Leave on one side.

2. Melt the butter in a frying pan, add the flour and stir until brown. Pour in the broth, white wine and milk and mix well. Add the stuffing. Season well with salt and pepper and bring to the boil.

3. Pour the mixture over the chicken and place in the oven at 180°C /350°F / Gas Mark 4 for one hour.

4. This is best served with creamed mash.

Hearty chicken curry

60g / 2oz ghee (clarified butter)
900g / 2lb chicken breast, skinless, boneless and sliced
2 medium onions, peeled and roughly chopped
3 cloves of garlic, crushed
2 teaspoons fresh ginger, finely chopped
1 teaspoon each of turmeric, cumin, curry powder and gram masala
1 teaspoon chillies, freshly chopped
1 can / 440g / 1lb chopped plum tomatoes
1 cup / 250ml / 9 fl oz chicken stock or water
2 cups / 500ml / 18 fl oz coconut cream
1 capsicum (green bell pepper), chopped
3 oriental (lady finer) egg plants, chopped
1 tablespoon cilantro (fresh coriander), chopped
salt & pepper

1. Heat 3 spoons of butter in a large frying pan. Add some of the chicken slices and cook until golden brown, remove and transfer to a plate. Repeat in batches with the remaining chicken slices.
2. Add the remaining butter, onion, ginger, garlic, chillies, curry powder, turmeric, cumin, gram masala to the pan and cook over medium heat, stirring until the onions softens and the spices become fragrant (about 5 minutes). Add the tomatoes, stock and the coconut cream. Bring to the boil.
3. Add the vegetables, reduce the heat and simmer uncovered for about 20 minutes.
4. Return the chicken to the pan and simmer for a further 10 minutes. Add the coriander and stir for another minute. Season to taste.
5. Serve in a bowl with rice and some accompaniments such as mango chutney, yoghurt, cucumber and mint, a bowl of sundried tomato salsa and a few poppadoms.

161

Poullet Epinard
(Spinach stuffed under chicken skin)

Serves 4

4 chicken breasts with skin attached
275g / 10oz fresh spinach, chopped, washed and drained
125g / 4oz water chestnuts, chopped
225g / 8oz cream cheese
1 cup sour cream
1 clove garlic, finely chopped
1 knob of butter
1 tablespoon olive oil
1 glass of white wine
seasoning

1.   Place the spinach, water chestnuts and cream cheese in a mixing bowl. Season with salt and pepper, then mix well and put aside.
2.   Place the oil and butter in a frying pan over a medium heat. Add the garlic and toss for 1 minute, then add the sour cream and white wine. Bring to the boil and remove from the heat.
3.   Lift the skin of each chicken from the neck and fill with the mixture.
4.   Place the chicken on an oven tray, pour the sauce over and cover with aluminium foil. Cook for 30 minutes in a pre-heated oven marked 180°C /350°F / Gas Mark 4.
5.   Remove the foil and place back in the oven for another 30 minutes.
6.   Serve immediately. Drizzle the sauce around it.

Hearty chicken casserole

2 tablespoons olive oil
2 kg / 4 ½ lb chicken pieces
2 onions, peeled and sliced lengthwise
2 cloves garlic, finely chopped
250g / 9oz thinly sliced prosciutto
3 carrots, thickly sliced
2 celery stalks, thickly sliced
400g / 14 oz canned chopped tomatoes
2 tablespoons tomato paste
1 cup water or chicken stock
400g / 14 oz cannelloni beans, rinsed and drained
2 tablespoons freshly chopped basil
2 tablespoons dried oregano
salt & pepper

1. Warm the oil in a large frying pan over a high heat. Add the chicken pieces and turn for 5 minutes until brown. Drain and transfer to a plate.

2. Use the same pan and reduce the heat to medium. Add garlic, onion, carrots, celery and prosciutto. Stir for 5 minutes until the onions are softened, add tomatoes and tomato paste together with the stock or water, bring to the boil.

3. Return the chicken pieces to the pan, reduce the heat and simmer uncovered until the chicken is cooked through (about 15 minutes). Add the beans and herbs and simmer for a further 3 minutes.

4. Garnish with fresh basil and serve immediately.

Hearty Chicken Couscous

1 tablespoon olive oil
1 medium onion, finely chopped
1 clove garlic, finely crushed
375g / 13 oz chicken thigh meat cut into 1" cubes
3 carrots, cut into 1" pieces
2 cups chicken stock or water
1 stalk celery, sliced
1 teaspoon turmeric
1 teaspoon cumin
1 teaspoon cayenne pepper
1 medium courgette (zucchini), cut into 1" strips
2 large tomatoes, peeled, seeded and chopped
1 can / 470g / 1 lb 1 oz chick peas or gazbanzo beans, drained
200g / 7oz couscous
1 tablespoon freshly chopped parsley

1. Warm the oil over a medium heat in a large, heavy based frying pan. Add onion and garlic and stir until tender but not brown. Meanwhile, add salt, turmeric, cumin, celery, carrots and stir for half a minute. Add the chicken.
2. Add cayenne pepper, stock or water and bring to the boil. Reduce the heat, cover the pan and simmer for 20 minutes.
3. Add the courgettes and chick peas and simmer for a further 10 minutes until the chicken is cooked through. Season with salt and pepper.
4. Read the instructions on the packet when making the couscous. Once this is ready, spoon it out into a dish and make hole in it. Pour the chicken in the middle and cover with sauce. Garnish with chopped parsley.

Lincoln Log of America

Serves 2

2 chicken breasts
2 cups of breadcrumbs
1 cup walnuts, chopped
½ cup of celery, chopped
1 cup of chopped onion
1 glass of dry white wine
2 tablespoons béchamel
2 tablespoons olive oil
seasoning

1.   Wash and mince the chicken, then season with salt and crushed black peppercorn. Cook with a little water for 5 minutes.

2.   Fry the walnuts, celery and onion. Then mix together the wine, béchamel, oil and seasoning

3.   Mix the chicken with all the other ingredients in a large bowl, season well, then form the mixture into logs of 3 inches long.

4.   Heat the oil in a frying pan and fry the logs. Remove, drain and place on a plate. Pour some sesame seeds over and drizzle olive oil around the chicken.

Chicken chasseur modern style

Serves 4

1 kg 350g / 3lb chicken (whole)
1 tablespoon oil
4 tablespoons butter
2 shallots, finely chopped
125g / ¼ lb button mushrooms, sliced
1 tablespoon plain flour
½ cup white wine
2 tablespoons Brandy
2 teaspoons tomato paste
1 cup chicken stock
1 tablespoon chopped tarragon
1 teaspoon chopped parsley
seasoning

1. Cut the chicken into 8 pieces, then heat the oil in a frying pan with half the butter and sauté the chicken. Pour off the excess fat.

2. Add the remaining butter to the pan. Cook over a moderate heat then add shallots and mushrooms and stir for one minute.

3. Add flour and stir for a further minute before pouring the stock and adding the wine, brandy and tomato paste. Bring to the boil, then reduce the heat and add the tarragon.

4. Return the chicken to the pan and simmer for a further 30 minutes. Decorate with a sprig of parsley.

5. This dish is normally served with croutons.

Pullet Vallee Dauge

Serves 4

1 kg 350g / 3lb whole chicken, cut into 8 pieces
2 eating apples, peeled and cored
1 tablespoon of lemon juice
4 tablespoon of butter
1 medium onion, finely chopped
½ celery stalk, finely chopped
1 tablespoon flour
1/3 cup Calvados or brandy
2 cups of chicken stock
1/3 cup cream fraiche

1. Dice a quarter of the apples and cut the rest into wedges. Pour lemon juice over them.
2. Heat half the butter in a large frying pan, cook both sides of the chicken, 5 minutes either side. Remove the chicken from the pan and pour off the fat.
3. Heat one tablespoon of butter in a frying pan. Add onion, celery and diced apples and stir for five minutes. Sprinkle the flour and stir for a further minute. Add brandy, chicken stock and chicken and cook for 15 minutes. Remove the chicken from the pan and pour off any excess fat from the sauce. Add crème fraiche. Bring to the boil and season.
4. Meanwhile, fry the apples wedges in a separate frying pan with the remaining butter until brown. Remove from the pan and keep warm.
5. Place the chicken in a serving dish, pour on the sauce and top with wedges.

167

Poulet à la Crème

Serves 4

225g / 8oz chicken breast
1 knob butter
2 tablespoons béchamel
dash of cream
½ glass of white wine
½ onion, diced
2 mushrooms, sliced
1 tablespoon olive oil
1 teaspoon cracked black pepper
pinch of salt and pepper

1. Pan fry the chicken breast in olive oil until cooked.

2. In another pan melt butter and sauté the onion on a low heat for 1
    minute. Add the mushrooms and stir until tender. Add the
    pepper, salt, wine, béchamel and cream, simmering until the
    sauce has reduced.

3. Place the chicken in the centre of the plate. Pour the sauce over
    and serve immediately.

Primer Coq Au Vin

Serves 8

2 x 1 kg 350g / 3lb chickens, each cut into 8 pieces
1 bottle red wine
2 bay leaves
2 thyme sprigs
225g / 8oz bacon rashers
6 tablespoons butter
20 shallots (pearl onions)
225g / 8oz button mushrooms
½ cup plain flour
4 cups chicken stock
½ cup brandy
2 teaspoons tomato paste
2 tablespoons chopped parsley

1. Place the chicken in a large bowl with red wine and thyme. Season well. Leave overnight to marinate.
2. Blanch the bacon. Cut and dry, then sauté in a frying pan with a quarter of the butter, onions and mushrooms. Season well and set aside.
3. Drain the chicken, making sure that the marinade is reserved. Place the chicken in a large frying pan, adding the remaining butter. Add stock, bay leaves, brandy and marinade together with the mushrooms, bacon, onion and tomato paste, then cook for 45-60 minutes.
4. If you need to thicken the sauce, add flour and butter. A few minutes before serving, add chopped parsley.

Hearty Coq Au Vin

4 slices French bread, cut into 1" pieces
3 cloves garlic, finely chopped
50g / 2 oz butter
4 tablespoons olive oil
1kg / 2lb 4oz chicken pieces
2 bacon rashers, finely diced
4 medium mushrooms, quartered
12 pickling onions, peeled
1 large tomato, seeded, peeled and chopped
2 tablespoons plain flour
2 tablespoons tomato paste
4 tablespoons parsley and tarragon, finely chopped
1 cup dry red wine
salt & pepper

1. Croutons: Place the bread cubes in a shallow baking dish and drizzle some olive oil with some crushed garlic. Place in the oven 150°C /300°F / Gas Mark 2 and turn only once after 15 minutes.
2. Increase the oven heat to180°C /350°F / Gas Mark 4 for the coq au vin. Place the chicken pieces in a large oven proof heavy based frying pan with the tomato over a medium heat and brown the chicken on all sides with some butter and olive oil.
3. Add the mushrooms, garlic, onion and bacon and cook until the onions are soft. Add the flour and cook stirring for a further minute.
4. Add the wine, stock or a little water, tomato paste, parsley, tarragon and season with salt and pepper. Bring to the boil and cover with aluminium foil and place in the oven for 45 minutes.
5. Before serving, remove excess fat and transfer to a serving dish. Crown with croutons and garnish with some parsley.

Chicken Cordon blue

Serves 4

4 large chicken cutlets or battered chicken fillet
4 thin slices turkey
125g / 4oz goats cheese
½ clove garlic, finely chopped
2 cups bread crumbs
2 cups plain flour
3 tablespoon olive oil
1 tablespoon finely chopped parsley
seasoning

1.   Spread the chicken cutlets in a tray. Put a slice of turkey in the centre of each chicken and put the tray to one side.

2.   Mash all the other ingredients in a mixing bowl and turn them into 4 even sized thick cigars but half as wide as the cutlets.

3.   Place each cigar in the middle of the turkey.

4.   Roll and tie a white thread round each chicken. Pan fry with olive oil to seal.

5.   Place the chicken in a 180°C /350°F / Gas Mark 4 oven and bake for 15 minutes.

6.   Serve immediately with freshly cooked vegetables.

Tandori Chicken

Serves 4

4 x 200-225g / 7-8 oz chicken breast, skinned and boned
½ cup mango chutney
4 portions basmati rice
poppadoms
spicy yoghurt marinade which includes:
     ½ cup plain yoghurt
     1 tablespoon lemon juice
     2 teaspoons grated ginger
     1 teaspoon paprika
     1 teaspoon coriander
     pinch ground cloves
     seasoning

1. Cut the chicken breasts into 2 inch pieces. Wash them and place in a bowl.

2. Mix the marinade ingredients well and pour over the chicken, then place in a refrigerator for at least one hour.

3. Put the chicken onto a tray and cook for 20 minutes. Turn the chicken, then cook for a further 20 minutes.

4. Serve immediately with basmati rice, mango chutney and poppadoms.

Modern Chicken Chasseur

Serves 4

4 x 225g / 8oz chicken breasts
4 knobs of butter
½ small onion, diced
2 mushrooms, sliced
1 clove garlic, crushed
1 glass dry white wine
3 tablespoons béchamel
splash of cream
pinch of salt & pepper
olive oil

1.   Pan fry the chicken with oil for 5 minutes on either side. Remove the excess fat, then add butter in the same pan together with the onion, mushrooms and garlic then fry until tender.

2.   Pour in the wine, béchamel and cream, then season and cook on a low heat for a further 6-7 minutes, until the sauce is reduced.

3.   This dish is best served with rice or vegetables.

Casseroles

There is something so brilliantly simple about making delicious dishes in a pot or a saucepan. It does not even matter if you overcook it or put extra herbs and spices into it. Potted dished can be made in advance and reheated later. In fact they often taste better if they are made ahead, and there is little washing up. Potted meals can be cooked in the oven or put on the stove and left entirely to themselves with added water, stock, cream or wine so, what are you waiting for? Let's roll:

Winter vegetable hotpot with courgettes and walnuts

500g / 18oz courgettes, thickly sliced
1 large onion, sliced
2 medium leeks trimmed and sliced
2 medium carrots, sliced 1 cm deep
2 medium turnips, peeled and sliced
50g / 2oz chopped roasted walnuts
2 tablespoons crème fraiche
2 tablespoons chopped fresh parsley
3 tablespoons olive oil
2 large bay leaves
knob of butter, melted
350g / 12oz vegetable stock (can be made with bouillon powder)
50g /2oz grated Parmesan or cheddar cheese
pinch of sea slat & grated black pepper

1. Heat the oven to180°C /350°F / Gas Mark 4. Tip all the vegetables into a saucepan or cast iron casserole pan except the courgettes. Add the bay leaves, oil and parsley, stir for a minute or two. Add the crème fraiche and stock and bring to the boil, then remove from the heat.

2. Grate the courgettes or make them into julienne strips. Put them into a large bowl together with the melted butter, cheese and walnut. Mix well and pour the mixture into the casserole on top of the other mixture. Put a sheet of foil over the dish without folding the foil over the edge.

3. Bake for about 20 minutes and then remove the foil. Leave to bake for another 15 minutes until brown. Allow to cool for 5 minutes before serving.

175

Lancashire hotpot with kidney and red wine

Serves 4

1kg / 2lb 4oz / 8 best end of neck lamb chops
4 lamb kidneys
2 large onions, quartered and sliced
500ml / 18fl oz lamb stock (could be made with bouillon powder)
2 large potatoes, peeled
50g / 2oz butter, melted
3 tablespoons olive oil
pinch dried rosemary
1 glass red wine
pinch of sea salt & freshly ground pepper

1. Heat the oven to 180°C /350°F / Gas Mark 4.
2. Trim excess fat from the chops. Sauté the chops in a frying pan to lightly brown then remove. Keep the oil.
3. Halve the kidneys, snip out the cores with scissors and then cut in half again. Place them in the same frying pan and sauté. Remove from the pan and keep with the lamb chops.
4. Put the onion and rosemary into the frying pan and fry until soft in the butter. Add the wine and stock and bring to the boil.
5. Place the lamb and the kidneys into the pan and the sliced potatoes then put into the oven for almost 1 hour, until the meat is tender and lightly crisp.
6. Remove and cool for 5 minutes before serving.

Iranian hotpot winter warmer
(Toss kebab)

2 large quince (or cooking apple), thickly sliced
2 large onions, thickly sliced
2 large potatoes, sliced ½ cm thick
4 large tomatoes, sliced
2 large mixed peppers, sliced
1 large egg plant, peeled and sliced
2 cloves garlic, crushed
1 tablespoon turmeric
1 teaspoon fresh ginger, finely chopped
1 teaspoon dried thyme
1 teaspoon dried mint or 10g fresh mint
600ml / 1 pint vegetable stock or water
3 tablespoons olive oil
1 tablespoon tomato puree
pinch sea salt & freshly ground pepper

1. Use a large saucepan if you are going to be cooking on the stove or an ovenproof dish for cooking in the oven.

2. Lay the ingredients layer by layer in order of onion, potato, quince, tomato and eggplant and peppers and repeat until all the ingredients are finished. Add water or stock to the pan. Let it come to the boil on the stove.

3. Sprinkle the ginger, turmeric, garlic, thyme and mint and let it boil for a few minutes. Stir in the tomato puree.

4. Remove and place in the oven for an hour or more until tender. Remove and let cool for 10 minutes before serving. This dish is normally served with salad and hot bread.

Recipes from other Kitchens

Having worked in various restaurants in the world, certain chefs always have their own particular way of doing certain dishes. Here are some of those recipes.

Langoustine and Clotted Cream Quiche with Tarragon and Parsley

Serves 6-8

For the pastry:
225g / 8oz plain flour
pinch of salt
65g / 2 ½ oz butter cut into pieces
65g / 2 ½ oz lard cut into pieces
1 cup water
1 egg white

For the filling:
750g / 1 lb 11 oz cooked langoustine in the shell
175 ml / 6 fl oz milk
100g / 3 ½ oz clotted cream
3 large eggs
1 tablespoon chopped parsley
1 tablespoon chopped tarragon
pinch of salt & pepper

1. For the pastry case, sift the flour and salt into a mixing bowl, add butter and lard. Mix well until it is like breadcrumbs.
2. Pre heat the oven to 200°C /400°F / Gas Mark 6. Add water to the mix and knead briefly until smooth. Make 4cm deep, 22cm flan tin and chill for 20 minutes.
3. Line the pastry case with a sheet of crumpled greaseproof paper and bake for 15 minutes then remove from the oven. Discard the paper and return to the oven for a further 5 minutes. Remove from the oven, brush with the unbeaten egg white and return to the oven for another minute.
4. After removing the pastry from the oven, reduce the heat to 190°C /375°F / Gas Mark 5. Remove the langoustine meat from the shell.
5. Gradually mix the milk into the clotted cream until smooth, beat in the eggs, then stir in the tarragon, parsley, salt and pepper.
6. Scatter the meat over the base of the pastry case, then pour over the egg mixture and bake in the oven for approximately 25 minutes, until golden brown.
7. Remove and cool slightly before serving.

179

Salmon with pink grapefruit hollandaise

Serves 4

4 x 120g / 4 oz Salmon fillets (with skin on)
2 tablespoons olive oil
2 tablespoons white wine vinegar
150g / 5 oz unsalted butter
1 pink grapefruit
1 free-range egg
5 coriander seeds, crushed
1 tablespoon chopped fresh coriander
1 tablespoon chopped fresh mint
sea salt & freshly ground pepper

1.	Boil down the vinegar to 1 tablespoon. This takes seconds.

2.	Melt the butter over a gentle heat. Pour off the oil into a jug and discard the milky solids. Set the oil aside to cool until tepid.

3.	Grate a teaspoon of grapefruit zest and set aside. Cut off the thick skin and white pith, then slicing between the membranes, cut out the segment. You need four segments for this sauce. Try to cut segments over the cup with the vinegar so that all the juice drips into the cup.

4.	Place the four large segments on a plate, use a fork to break the flesh into tiny pieces. Set aside.

5.   Put the yolks, crushed coriander and a tablespoon of cold water into a heat proof bowl that will fit snugly over a pan of gently simmering water.

6.   Using a hand held blender or electric whisk, beat the egg whites over the heated water until light and frothy. This helps the butter emulsify more easily.

7.   Remove the bowl form the heat and continue to whisk for a couple more minutes, then slowly trickle in the tepid runny butter as you continue to whisk. Do not add the butter too quickly or it will curdle.

8.   When all the butter is incorporated, season and add the vinegar, any juices and grapefruit zest plus the tiny pieces of grapefruit flesh. Fold in the coriander and mint. Set the bowl back over the pan of hot water, but off the heat and stir occasionally to stop any skin forming. This will keep it soft.

9.   When ready to serve, brush the salmon with the oil. Heat a large non-stick frying pan until you can feel a strong heat rising. Lay the salmon fillet in skin side down and turn the heat to medium. Season the flesh and cook for five minutes on the skin, which should become quite crisp. Flip the fish over and cook for another 3 minutes until slightly springy. Remove. Allow 5 minutes before serving with the warm sauce.

Smoke Haddock Risotto Cake

Serves 4-6

300g / 11oz filet smoked haddock
500ml / 18 fl oz skimmed milk
1 onion, finely diced
1 clove garlic, crushed
200g / 7oz Arborio risotto rice
3 tablespoons breadcrumbs
100g / 3 ½ oz baby spinach leaf
50g / 2 oz grated Parmesan cheese
2 medium eggs, separated
2 tablespoons olive oil
2 tablespoons Mascarpone cheese
1 vegetable stock cube
1 teaspoon Curry powder / turmeric
sea salt & freshly ground pepper

1. Cut the fillet in half, place in a large pan with milk and bring to the boil. Remove from the heat and leave to cool. Reserve the liquid and scoop the fish out onto a plate making sure there are no stray bones after the skin has been pulled off. Flake the flesh into small chunks.

2. Place the onion, garlic, turmeric or curry powder in a large saucepan and fry in the olive oil for 2-3 minutes until soft.

3. Use a round cake tin 20-23 cm diameter and 3-4 cm deep. Brush with melted butter then toss in the breadcrumbs. Shake well to coat the base and sides evenly and tip out the remains.

4. Add the rice to the curried onion with the milk and the same amount of water and let it boil, adding the stock cube, stirring frequently until the liquid is completely absorbed.

5. Add the spinach into the pan and stir until it wilts in the heat, then add the fish and mascarpone and mix well. Season and let it cool for 10 minutes. Beat in the egg yolks.

6. Beat the egg whites until firm and pour into the mixture in the pan. Scoop into the tin and bake in a preheated oven 180°C /350°F / Gas Mark 4 for 20-25 minutes until the centre is lightly set and golden brown.

7. Remove and cool for 5 minutes, then run a table knife around the edge and turn out. Add Parmesan.

Dover sole and Tarragon cream

Serves 2

2 Dover sole (300-350g / 11-12 oz), skinned
100g / 3 ½ oz butter for greasing
50g / 2 oz freshly chopped tarragon
good pinch of cayenne pepper
good pinch of ground mace
250ml / 9 fl oz double cream
juice of 1 lemon
pinch of salt

1.   Pre heat the oven to 230°C /450°F / Gas Mark 8 .

2.   Place the Dover sole side by side, slightly over lapping if
     necessary, in a buttered shallow baking dish and sprinkle with
     some salt, cayenne pepper and mace.

3.   Pour the cream over the fish and bake for 10-12 minutes, by
     which time the fish should be cooked through and the cream
     reduced and thickened.

4.   Carefully transfer the fish to warmed serving plates. Stir the
     lemon juice and chopped tarragon into the cream sauce. Adjust
     the seasoning to taste and pour over the fish.

Baked Fennel and Cavalo Nero with Anchovies, Capers and Parmesan

Serves 4

1-2 heads (500g / 1 lb 2 oz) of Cavalo nero (Italian black cabbage)
2 bulbs of fennel
150ml / 5 fl oz extra virgin olive oil
2 cloves garlic, peeled and crushed
2 tablespoons capers
50g / 2 oz can anchovies in olive oil, drained
2 tablespoons freshly grated Parmesan cheese
pinch salt & freshly ground pepper.

1. Put the fennel in the pan. Cover with salted water. Bring to the boil and simmer for 35-40 minutes until tender to the point of the knife. Remove from the heat and drain in a colander.
2. Remove the stalks from the cavalo nero, chop the leaves into mouth size pieces, wash in cold water and drain.
3. Cook in boiling salted water for 15-20 minutes until tender, then drain in a colander.
4. Pre heat the oven to 180°C /350°F / Gas Mark 4.
5. Mix the garlic and half the olive oil with the cavalo nero and season with salt and pepper and lay it in the bottom of an ovenproof dish.
6. Cut each fennel into 6 pieces and lay them on top of the cavalo nero.
7. Season with salt & pepper spooning over the rest of the olive oil.
8. Cover with a lid or foil and bake in the oven for 40 minutes.
9. Remove the lid, arrange the anchovies over the fennel and scatter the capers on top.
10. Sprinkle the Parmesan cheese and return to the oven for another 15 minutes before serving.

Prawn Teppanyaki

6 King prawns
1 tablespoon sake
1 tablespoon soy
2 tablespoons yuzu sauce
15g / ½ oz 1 tablespoon grated onion
5g / 1 teaspoon freshly chopped garlic
30g / 1 ½ oz freshly chopped parsley
knob butter
pinch salt & pepper

1.   Sauté ingredients except parsley with butter on a teppan table or flat top until golden brown.

2.   Add parsley one minute before serving.

3.   Serve with a mixed sauté of vegetables, bean sprouts, shitake and button mushrooms.

Roasted Quail and Five Spice Marinade

Serve 2

4 oven ready quails

For the stuffing:
- 4 spring onions, trimmed and cut roughly in 4
- 3 garlic cloves, crushed
- 1 thumb of ginger, grated

For the marinade:
- 3 tablespoons of Sake or dry sherry
- 2 tablespoons oyster sauce
- 1 tablespoon Japanese soy sauce
- 1 tablespoon Sesame oil
- 3 pinches five-spice powder
- 2 pinches caster sugar
- 2 dashes sweet chilli sauce
- pinch salt & pepper

1. Put the quail in a small, non-reactive dish. Whisk the marinade ingredients together and set aside. Combine the stuffing ingredients and chop coarsely. Dab the mixture inside the birds, pour over the marinade and leave in a fridge for 4 hours turning occasionally.
2. Pre heat the oven to 230°C /450°F / Gas Mark 8. Remove the birds from the marinade, then put them on a large double sheet of aluminium foil and season well. Cover with the foil but ensure they are loosely wrapped and cook in the oven for 15 minutes. Meanwhile, pour the marinade into a small saucepan and boil it over a high heat uncovered, until it is shiny and slightly sticky.
3. Spread open or remove the foil, brush the quail with the marinade, continue to roast for 15 minutes or more until the birds are glistening brown.
4. Pour any juices in the foil back in to the marinade, spoon it over the birds and serve with salad.

Roasted Halibut with Wilted Lettuce and Fenugreek Broth

Serves 4

500ml / 18 fl oz fish stock
½ teaspoon Fenugreek seeds (methi)
4 little gem lettuces
500ml bottle pure olive oil (not extra virgin)
4 x 125g / 4 oz thick cut fillet fresh halibut, skinned
4 tablespoons white vinaigrette
½ large red chilli, seeded and sliced thinly
¼ large onion, sliced thinly
extra virgin olive oil to drizzle
sea salt and freshly ground black pepper

1. Boil the fish stock with the fenugreek seeds until reduced by half, then strain, check the seasoning and set aside.
2. Remove the outer leaves of lettuces until you reach the inner core. Heat about 3 tablespoons of olive oil in a large shallow pan and sauté the leaves gently until wilted. Pour in the stock and add seasoning. Bring to the boil and then simmer for 3 minutes until the stock is reduced by a third. Set aside.
3. Place the remaining oil in a medium frying pan to a depth that will cover the fish, then heat it for about two minutes. Slide the halibut steak into the fat (bear in mind you are poaching the fish and not frying it) for about 5 minutes until the flesh is firm.
4. Remove and drain, then heat a non-stick frying pan until it feels quite hot and cook the fish quickly on each side until light brown. Remove the pan from the heat.
5. Season the lettuce and toss in the vinaigrette, chilli and onion and divide between 4 plates. Place a halibut steak on top and drizzle any lettuce juice around. Serve, drizzled with a little extra virgin olive oil.

Menu Suggestions

Evening menu

Starters

Duckling pasta
Tagliatelle with strips of duckling and wild mushroom finished
With cream, basil and emmenthal cheese

Prawn, scallop & bacon salad
Served with ginger, lime and galliano dressing

Samun mousse
Smoked salmon mousse with spinach coulis and brown bread

Main course

Grilled sea bass with fennel
Fillet of sea bass marinated in balsamic vinegar and fennel
served with black pepper and lemon

Pork fillet with calvados
Pork fillet stuffed with raisins, walnuts and calvados cream

Lamb, lime and rosemary marmalade
Rack of lamb baked with fresh lime and rosemary marmalade

Chef's special Spring menu

Spiced apple and parsnip soup
With granary wedges, bread dough and aubergine gratin

Lemon chicken
Strips of chicken fillet marinated in fresh lemon juice, pan fried
And bedded on mixed leaves and blue cheese dressing

Celery and stilton terrine
On a bed of melon with caramelised orange dressing and melba toast

Calamari
Deep fried fresh squid rings on a bed of tomato slices with balsamic
vinegar and lemon wedges

Main course

Turkey salvia
Slices of turkey saddle pan fried with garlic butter with onion and
sage enhanced with cream and white wine, nested on fried leeks

Entrecote foresteir
Sirloin steak grilled to your liking and topped with a sauce of
bacon, spring onion, garlic, peppers and fresh tomato bedded on
tarragon mash

Poulet à la kiev
Breast of chicken stuffed with garlic butter, coated in bread
crumbs baked in oven and nested on glazed spinach

Cod parsil
Pan fried cod fillet in a sauce of onion, parsley, cream and
white wine on a bed of basil mash

Early Fall Menu

Starters

Fenoil avec sauce aux tomates
Fennel bulbs oven baked in rich tomato basil dressing

Paquet de epinard aux choux
Stuffed cabbage with spinach, capers and feta cheese in a sauce of garlic and walnut cream

Cream of leek and potato soup
Cream of leek & potato soup with bread dough croutons, shaved Parmesan cheese, fried leeks and Granary bread

Main course

Black butter skate
Roasted skate wings with mustard butter and toasted bread crumbs on carrot mash

Sword fish pacific
Pan fried sword fish with chopped spring onion and julienne of smoked salmon on watercress sauce

Der mullett pampano
Baked whole red mullet served on tartare potato cake, crowned with soft baked egg

Bream papillote
Fresh bream oven baked in an envelope with chopped spring onion, mixed peppers and fresh lemon tomato herb, prawns and white wine

Chef's Special Fish of the Day

King prawns aioli
Butterfly king prawns, pan fried in garlic butter and chopped parsley, enhanced with the juice of fresh lemon and served with classic orange rice

Marlin and salmon sauce with glazed cabbage
Marlin steak grilled, bedded on a glazed cabagge and crowned with a sauce of smoked salmon and anchovy cream

Sword fish, seared orange and braised leek
Sword fish steak oven baked in a traditional manner with lemon butter and bedded on a grilled melon with braised leeks and seared orange dressing

Craftsman Cod with Prawn Gravy
Fresh cod roasted and served on a bed of creamed mash with roasted potatoes and prawn gravy

Escolar Béarnaise and cockles
All meat escalor steak oven baked on a bed of noodles and topped with a sauce of tarragon wine vinegar, mustard and cream, crowned with cockles and flamed in brandy

Grilled Red Snapper
Succulent red snapper simply grilled and served on mixed leaves with balsamic vinegar dressing and lime wedges

Dover sole and anchovy crem with capers
Buttered and grilled Dover sole topped with a sauce of diced spring onions, anchovies, capers, cream and white wine, flamed in brandy

Moules Meuniere
Shell on mussels pan fried with spring onion, garlic, freshly chopped basil in a sauce of white wine and cream

John Dory with lemon butter
A superb deep sea fish is oven baked and served with linguini pasta and lemon butter dressing

Table d'hote Menu
du chef Novita

Primo

Potage aux choux
Cabbage soup with bacon, parsnip, leek, celery and stilton cheese

Buletts de lemon
Melon balls in a sauce of orange and port

Pate au saumongalantine
salmon pate made with white wine and brandy

Salade de mer
seafood salad including prawns, squid, mussels, cockles and tuna

Principal

Poulet le monseigneur
Chicken breast flattened and stuffed with cheese, Parma ham and
garlic butter, rolled and coated in bread crumbs
and oven baked until golden

Filet de veau au paprika
Trimmed fillet of veal sautéed with butter, bacon, onions and
paprika in a cream sauce

Entrecote Diana
Fillet steak flattened and coated with French mustard, pan fried with
diced onion and mushroom in a cream and brandy sauce

Le saint laurent crevettes
Butterfly king prawns shallow fried in garlic butter and chives and
brought into perfection with a dash of fresh lemon juice

Mothering Sunday

APPETISERS

Soup de jour
Cream of spiced apple and celery with aubergine gratin shaved
Parmesan and granary wedges

Bullets de melon
Melon balls with sweet sherry and mandarin segments

Salmon and watercress roulade
Poached salmon with watercress in a ramakin dish served
with the fruit of the field

Duck and mushroom pate
A coarse pate made with mushrooms, garlic, duck and port,
served with finger toast.

MAIN COURSES

Du boeuf ou du porc ou un gignot d'agneau a'la bourguignon
Medallion of beef, pork, or lamb in a sauce of onion,
Mushrooms and red wine

Le creveete de rouille
Spiced king prawns with prawns and olives in a sauce of
tomato and thyme served with dill rice

Halibut aux ananas
Halibut steak panfried with butter and onion in a sauce of apple,
syrup and white wine on a bed of pineapple

Sweets
Bread and butter pudding - Hot pudding with brandy sauce
Fresh fruit salad - with fresh cream

St. Valentine's Day

Starters

Cupids cup
Soup of the day with granary wedges and shaved Parmesan cheese

Star of love
Stilton and celery terrine on mixed leaves, pepper coulis and
melba toast

Sweet me Duck
Warm pieces of duck breast with caramelised apple dressing

Porcheotto melon et crevetts
Melon and Parma ham served with prawns,
Maria rose and brown Bread

Champignon
Pan fried mushrooms with garlic, thyme, tomato and cheese

Main course

Chicken Venus
Breast of chicken stuffed with Parma ham and cheese, breaded and
served on glazed spinach and garlic butter dressing

Stincotto
Succulent lamb shank enhanced with rosemary, red wine and
Garlic butter dressing on a bed of basil mash

Fillet aux saglia
Fillet of beef pan-fried with onion, sage, white wine and cream,
flamed in brandy

Saucy red snapper
This special fish is highly seasoned and is served on a bed of creamed
mash with red wine and balsamic vinegar dressing

Onion parfait
Baked stuffed onion with seasoned vegetables, topped with
cream cheese and served on a bed of dill rice

Dessert
Strawberries and cream

Tapas

Spinach wrap
Tortilla wrapped around spinach, potato, walnut,
onion and feta cheese

Prawn aioli
Tiger prawns with garlic butter, chopped with
fresh parsley and lemon juice

Dolmatos
Vine leaves stuffed with rice, mince beef and lentils, then dusted
with sesame seeds and tarragon oil

Kofta
Turkish style rice balls with chickpeas, celery and coriander

Baby calamari
Stuffed with rice, anchovy, lime and dill

Crostini ricotta
French bread brushed with chilli oil and crushed garlic

Crostini mediterranean
Roasted vegetables

Salmon with avocado salsa
Diced salmon and salsa, crowned with a tower of curly endive

Roasted tomato and mushrooms
With garlic and chilli oil dressing

All Day Bar Menu

LIGHTER BITES
Garlic bread to share
Garlic bread and cheese to share
Hot pesto bread to share
French fries to share
Avocado salad and Italian dressing
Salad Nicoise
Potato wedges and dips

LIGHT BITES
Brie parcels
French brie wedges in filo pastry crowned with gooseberry sauce
Fungi Toscana
Toasted mushrooms in garlic butter with tomato and thyme
Feta and spinach wrap
Glazed spinach with feta and walnut wrapped in pancakes
Bruschetta marmalade
Ciabatta bread coated with garlic butter, topped with goat cheese
and onion marmalade

SANDWICHES
Ham and wholegrain mustard
Chicken and sun dried tomato salsa
Salmon dill and garlic mayo
Cheddar, mayo and spring onion
Zucchini and humus
Baguettes
Bacon and brie
Steak, fried onion and mushroom
Copidyka or minced lamb kebab

Bar Lunch Menu

SANDWICHES
Mature cheddar cheese
Tuna mayonnaise
Prawns and marie-rose sauce
Home-baked ham and wholegrain dijon mustard

SPECIALITY SANDWICHES
Chicken, bacon, lettuce and tomato club sandwich
served with crisps
Coronation chicken with sultanas and toasted almonds,
served on honey and sunflower seed bread
Hungarian banger baguette, mixed sausages served with
Dijon mustard and pickled cucumber
Hot marinated steak baguette with sautéed mushrooms
and onion, served with chips

TRADITIONAL
Char grilled ham, free range eggs and chips
Cheese topped cottage pie served with chips
Curry of the day
A smaller portion of freshly battered cod and chips

LIGHTER BITES
Fisherman's triple salad platter of tuna mayonnaise,
Freshly Poached salmon and chilled prawns, served with
marie-rose Sauce and fresh bread
Warm sautéed mushrooms, served on a mixed salad with
garlic and herb dressing and lightly fried croutons
Hot jacket potato filled with coronation chicken,
sultanas and almonds
Hot jacket potato filled with vegetarian chilli
Hot jacked potato filled with tuna mayonnaise, topped
with melted cheese

A'la Carte Menu

Avocado Mediterranean
Fan of avocado embellished with tuna served with a cream cheese
sauce

Salmon and watercress roulade
Freshly poached salmon cooked with watercress in a ramekin dish
and served with fruits of the field

Duck and mushroom pate
A coarse pate served with melba toast

MAIN COURSE

Escalope of pork chesterfield
Tender pork served in a sauce of green peppercorn and cream

Duke of Westminster lamb
Noisettes of lamb gently grilled and served on a bed of spinach
encased with smoked salmon amply enhanced with
a white wine and cheese sauce

Entrecote mirabeal
Succulent 8oz sirloin cooked to your liking and served with
asparagus and olives

Fillet Budapest
Medallion of fillet (7oz) dusted with paprika and chilli,
served with a brandy and mushroom sauce

Lamb cutlets Louisiana
Tender diced cutlets, 1lb in weight, gently sautéed in ginger, garlic,
cumin and port in a red wine dressing

Anniversary Dinner for two

If I had to entertain my partner on our anniversary at home, I would probably be nervous that perfection may be expected, but I am only human! For this reason, I must have a perfect solution, which provides not only a relaxed atmosphere but something that would not be forgotten for years to come. This is the only way I could mark the occasion.

To begin

Cream of leek and potato soup with truffle oil, ravioli and buttered brown bread

To follow

Smoked salmon with Norwegian prawns on lolo roso leaves with asparagus tips, roasted pine nuts and blue cheese dressing

To continue

Fillet of beef pan fried in garlic butter, green pepper corns, diced onion and cream, flamed with brandy on a bed of wilted spinach and served with roasted cherry tomatoes and braised leeks with rosemary potatoes.

To finish

Fresh oranges in caramel sauce and toffee ice cream

Chinese Dinner

There are a fascinating range of Chinese dishes which can easily be prepared. The method of their cooking and their techniques, as well as their type of ingredients and vegetables are different. Once you have mastered one or two basic principles, you'll appreciate the speed and ease in which Chinese food can be cooked. I have chosen a selection of my favourites for you to try.

Starters

Chicken satay & stir-fry vegetables

Skewer of chicken fillet marinated in satay sauce grilled and nested on julienne of peppers, mange tout, leeks and courgettes in soy sauce.

Sweet & sour pork with noodles

Strips of pork fillet pan fried with finely diced onion in a sauce of sweet and sour sauce and bedded on noodles.

Sizzled chilli prawns with sherry

Marinated king prawns in soy sauce and dry sherry with chillies, garlic, cashews, spring onion, and ginger are fried in a wok or frying pan to bring into a shiny glaze and served with or without basmati wild rice.

Spiced scallops

Wok fried spring onions, garlic, ginger and mange tout tossed with scallops, sherry, soy sauce and honey with sesame seeds.

Main course

Baked trout with black bean sauce

Rainbow trout oven baked with butter, crowned with black bean sauce
on a bed of tiger lily and bamboo shoots.

Chicken chop soy

Shredded chicken fillets, wok stir fried with bean sprouts, julienne of
peppers and carrots, highly seasoned with wine and soy sauce.

Beef & bok choy

Wok fried strips of beef with spring onions, mange tout, baby (dwarf)
corn, red peppers with garlic and sugar served
on a bed of steamed bok choy leaves.

Five spice lamb

Lamb pieces are wok fried with five spice powder with bell peppers,
spring onion, French or runner beans in a sauce of sherry
and soy with coriander.

Duck with pineapple

Wok fried chopped spring onions, carrots and ginger with strips of
skinless duck breast in a sauce of pineapple chunks and syrup.

Fathers Day Dinner

Primo

Cream de broccoli et stilton a' la ciboulette
Cream of broccoli and stilton soup garnished with chives

Oeuf poche sur feauillete de foie de volailles
Sauté chicken liver topped with poached egg

Sautee de gambas aioli
Butterfly king prawns in salted garlic

Principal

Supreme de poulet aux epices et au poireaux
Chicken breast laced with chilli, surrounded with leeks julienne

Croustillant de canard au gingember
Crispy duck with spring onion and ginger

Sauté de lotte à la puree d' onion citronnee
Wok seared monkfish with onion and lemon marmalade

Cotelettes d'Agneau à la groseille et romarin
Lamb cutlets with redcurrant and rosemary sauce

Curry de legumes et son riz à la noix de coco
Vegetable curry and coconut rice

Cuisine de la Nouvelle France

Hors d' oeuvre

Soupe à l oignon
French onion soup served with bread dough croutons and Parmesan

Cocktail de epinard
Glazed spinach with onion and garlic, topped with minted yoghurt on
sliced tomatoes and served with melba toast.

Buletts de riz avec sauce aux tomates
Savoury rice balls in a sauce of tomato, garlic, thyme and white wine.

Pate au poulet et legumes parfait
Chicken liver pate with brandy and port and served
with toasted walnut bread.

Mosaique de carottes et d'avocats
A distinctive terrine of carrots and avocado mosaic with
yellow pepper coulis and granary bread.

Farci aux choux avec formage et capers
Stuffed cabbage with feta cheese and capers served
with pickled peppers.

Gingember de crevetts avec sauce barbecue
King prawns coated in garlic and ginger bread crumbs and
served with B.B.Q. sauce.

Champignons frits
Baked breaded mushrooms in garlic butter on curly endive.

Salade de mer
Seafood salad with prawns, cockles, mussels, squid and tuna
on a bed of mixed leaves and toasted garlic bread.

Snails in garlic butter and coriander
Oven baked and served with light garlic bread wedges.

Frog legs in garlic butter and chopped parsley
Pan fried frogs legs in garlic butter with white wine, lime and parsley
with roasted cherry tomatoes.

Principal

Riz au spaghetti– servi avec legumes, de la mer, viande au a'la creme
Rice or spaghetti served with the choice of vegetables, seafood, meat
or cream sauce with light French garlic bread .

French Cuisine

Repas Principal

Poulet le monseigneur
Breast of chicken stuffed with Parma ham, cheese and garlic butter,
rolled and coated with breadcrumbs and pan fried,
served on a bed of lemon rice.

Poulet à la cream
Pan fried chicken supreme with onion and mushrooms in a sauce of
cream and white wine, served with dill rice.

Poulet le roulade
Flattened breast of chicken stuffed with glazed onion,
garlic and spinach pan fried and nesting on a tarragon sauce

Canard à la bigarade
Duck breast pan fried and bedded on a sauce of orange, lemon
and white wine, flamed with cherry brandy.

Canard à la saint louie
Pan fried duck breast in a sauce of black cherries, red current jelly
and red wine dressing on a bed of noodles.

Entrecote forestiera
Pan fried sirloin steak in a sauce of diced onion, bacon,
peppers and garlic with tomato, potato and basil.

Entrecote Diane

Pan fried sirloin steak diced onions, mushrooms,
French mustard and cream flamed in brandy.

Filet de boeuf au paprika

Fillet of beef pan fried with diced onions and bacon seasoned
with paprika in a cream and brandy sauce.

Filet de boeuf au poivre

Pan fried fillet of beef in a sauce of diced onion,
crushed black pepper corn with cream and brandy.

Moule mariner

Shelled mussels cooked in garlic, spring onion and
basil in a sauce of cream and white wine.

Une limande sauce à la mornay

Fillet of lemon sole pan fried with butter, diced shallots,
chives and dill in a sauce of cream and white wine.

Parfait voie de cuisson aubergine

Baked stuffed eggplant with mushrooms, walnut,
garlic and whey on a bed of cheese sauce.

Greek Dinner

When it comes to lamb and kebabs and mazes you find there is similarity between Greeks, Turks and Persians. They all have a passion for food and if you happen to be a female you must be able to cook otherwise you remain single for the rest of your life - this is how it goes over there!

As for me, I just love everything about them especially their respect for food. The recipes below are the ones with which I have always treated myself. Even the thought of them makes me hungry.

STARTERS

Garithes yigantes
King prawns in garlic butter and served on a bed of leaves.

Keftethes
Greek meatballs served on a bed of tomato and parsley dressing.

Dolmathes
Vine leaves stuffed with minced meat, rice, lentile and herbs.

Manitaria yemista
Mushrooms stuffed with feta cheese and garlic on a bed
of cream and white wine.

Hallumi and lounza
Pan fried feta and smoked bacon with eggs on a bed of rocket leaves
with olives and chillies.

Horiatiki

This is a Greek salad with olives and lemon dressing.

Mezethakia

A selection of Greek dips served with pita bread and that includes:

Taramosolata

Roe fish salad

Houmous

Chickpeas dip with olive oil and lemon juice and garlic.

Tzatziki

Greek yoghurt with cucumber, garlic and mint.

MAIN COURSE

Kleftico

Lamb knuckle with herbs and spices on garlic mash potato.

Souvlaki

Broiled pieces of lamb, chicken and pork kebab on a bed of rice.

Mousakka

The classic dish of aubergines, courgettes and potatoes on a bed of savoury minced beef topped with béchamel and cheese.

Pavidakia

Grilled lamb cutlets with fresh mint and mixed salad.

Indian Dinner

If you set out for the first time to cook Indian food, one has to cope with both the type of dish and the ingredients. Indian food is a favourite of mine that I love to cook and especially to eat

Starters

Pakoras

Ring onion, broccoli quarters and sliced potatoes, battered in a paste of gram masala, gram flour and cumin and deep fried.

King prawn bhuma

King prawns pan fried with onion and garlic, chillies, turmeric and paprika with the juice of fresh lemon.

Lamb & tomato koftas

Grilled skewer of meat balls made of minced lamb, fresh mint, onion, garlic and garam masala with tomato quarters.

Spicy fish and potato fritters

Soufflé of eggs, mash potato and minced cod with spring onion, chillies garlic and curry paste coated in bread crumbs and fried in butter.

Main course

King prawn biryani

Pan fried king prawns with coconut milk and yoghurt, highly spiced and served with raisin rice, spring onion and toasted almonds.

Lamb tikka masala

Potted lamb pieces with garlic, ginger, cumin, turmeric, chillies, mustard and fresh mint and coriander in yoghurt, coconut milk and fresh tomato served with basmati rice.

Chicken jalfrezi

Pieces of chicken fillets pan fried with onion, garlic, chillies, diced peppers, mustard seeds, turmeric and cumin with chopped tomato, garam masala and broad beans served with boiled rice.

Vindaloo beef curry

Pieces of beef fried in garlic, ginger, coriander, turmeric, potato and tomatoes with brown sugar mixed with a paste of vinegar, cloves, mustard seeds, cardamom, cinnamon, onion and cumin served with mango chutney, basmati rice and popadoms.

Italian Dinner

In the past 20 years Italian food has become popular among the young and old due to its simplicity, healthier diet and cheap ingredients as well as fast cooking techniques. There are fascinating recipes and here is my choice of recipes for you.

Anti – pasta

Zuppa alla ministrone
Vegetable soup served with Italian bread

Gamberetti maria rosa
Norwegian prawns crowned with maria rose sauce on a bed of mixed leaves with buttered brown bread

Funghi alla tscana
Pan fried mushrooms with garlic, onion and thyme in a sauce of white wine and fresh tomato served on fried bread

Pate della casa
Beef liver pate with garlic, brandy and port served with finger toast

Calamare
Deep fried squid rings with lemon wedges.

Pizza & pasta

Pizza
Italian base thin pan topped with tomato, cheese and oregano.

Lasagna
Layers of pasta sheets with minced meat, béchamel, cheese, eggs and
tomato sauce topped with grated Parmesan cheese.

Pasta or risotto bolognaise and carbonara - di mare
Any pasta dried or fresh with meat sauce, cream sauce
or seafood sauce.

Main course

Bistecca di manzo alla pizaiola
Pan fried sirloin steak with garlic, capers,
olives, tomato, white wine and oregano.

Filetto alla bascaiola
Pan fried fillet steak with chopped onion and
mushrooms in a red wine dressing.

Polo alla valdostana
Chicken supreme wrapped in bacon, oven baked
and topped with béchamel and cheese.

Salmone al limone
Poached Scottish salmon topped with prawns, capers and shallots
in a sauce of white wine and lemon dressing.

Japanese Dinner

Due to the fact that Japan is surrounded by water, most people rely on the sea for their major source of protein.   Japan shares some of its ingredients with China, but it has a distinctly different cuisine. Japanese do less stir frying and more steaming and simmering. Japanese starters are mostly pickled vegetables and as they are very inventive in cooking, more time is spent on preparation than cooking. If I happen to go for Japenese food I would certainly choose from the most popular dishes.

To begin

Tempura
Fish and vegetable fritters on a bed of
shredded chicory and lemon wedges.

Horenso tamago maki
Spinach omelette roll with nasu no karashi or fried aubergines.

Sashimi
Slices of raw fish such as sea bass together with king prawns
on a platter with freshly cut vegetables served with horseradish,
ginger and soy sauce separately in a bowl.

Kyuri to kani sunomono
Crab meat and diced cucumber are blended together in rice vinegar
with lemon rind and sesame seeds.

To follow

Prawns with spinach and water chestnut
Wok fried king prawns with chopped celery, onion and spinach in a sauce of soy, water chestnut, stock and cornstarch.

Beef tariyaki
Marinated tiny sliced fillet of beef in soy sauce, ginger, garlic and red wine Char grilled and served with a sauce of lemon juice and vinegar.

Nizakana
Braised salmon with sliced onion in a sauce of rice wine, soy sauce, sugar and ginger.

Persian Dinner

Ingredients used in Persian cooking are available in most chain stores. Persian foods are mildly spiced in contrast to the highly spiced curries of India.   Polou or chelou, which form the basis of both rice, is the main and the most traditional dish in all Persia.

Not only do Persian dishes vary from one section of the country to another, but from family to family. I can only offer you the most popular and easy to follow recipes.

Pish ghaza

Eshkaneh
Meatless soup with onion, eggs, potatoes and mint
This is served with naan bread

Kashk-o-bademjan
A blend of aubergines, whey, walnuts, garlic and minted butter

Kookoo sabzi
A light soufflé of eggs and fresh herbs with freshly made naan

Astera caviar
Fish eggs from the Caspian sea on a bed of fresh tomato with finely chopped eggs and onion

Barbecue

Makhsoos
Skewers of minced lamb with either lamb fillet pieces or baby chicken
marinated in lime juice and saffron served on a bed of
chelou rice and grilled tomatoes

Khoreshes

Qormeh sabzi
A combination of lamb shanks, chopped onion, celery, spinach,
parsley, dill and green onion leaves (leeks) casserole
with dried lime and served with polou rice

Qameh bademjoon
A casserole made of lamb leg, lentil and aubergines with tomato
and dried lime served with polou rice

Specials

Baghala polou ba goshet
Rice with broad beans and dill, accompanied by
potted lamb knuckle or chicken fillet

Zereshk polou ba morgh
Barberries rice and chicken fillet with saffron and
crowned with drizzled butter

Plat de Jour Dish of the Day

Primo

Canapes aux crevettes
Toasted white bread topped with Norwegian prawns, covered
in marie rose and surrounded by cream potatoes and brown bread

Concombres à la danoise
Salmon and hard boiled egg chopped and bedded on cucumber
topped with garlic mayonnaise and dill, surrounded by tomato slices

Boucheea à la reine
Vol-au-vent filled diced chicken, mushrooms and egg yolks flavoured
with Dijon mustard and lemon juice, on a bed of celery wedges

Principal

Saumon froid au beurre de montpellier

Scottish Salmon fillet poached in mixed fresh tarragon, parsley and
watercress and oven baked in butter with onion, gherkins, capers,
garlic and anchovies, bedded on spinach leaves,
topped with cut crescents of truffles and surrounded
by hard boiled egg slices

Truites avec sauce persil

Rainbow trout baked in the oven with butter and lime, served on a
bed of leeks and covered with fine white breadcrumb sauce

Plaice à la Florentine

Fillet of plaice, fried with butter and chopped spring onions in a sauce
of cream, beurre manie and chablis, topped with grated cheese and
bedded on wild basmati rice

Une limande avec sauce à la rochelaise

Lemon sole poached in fume de poisson and demi glace butter, onions
and Bordeaux, bedded on mixed poached mussels, cockles and prawns

Monkfish, sauce à la Veronique

Monkfish fillet pan fried with fume de poisson and court bouillon
au vin blanc and topped with grapes, peeled and pipped

General Tips for Caterers

Costing Sheet

Here is an example of a costings sheet that can be used when required:

Menu Item:				Date:	
Ingredients	Specification	Supplier code	Portion size	Unit Cost	Portion Cost

	Complete cost	
A	Cost per portion	
B	Minimum (Target) GP%	
C	Minimum Sales Price	
D	Actual Sales Price	
E	'Net' Sales Price	
F	Potential Cash Gross Profit	
G	Potential GP%	

Calculations:

$$\frac{A}{100-B} \times 1.175 = C$$

$$D + 1.175 \text{ (VAT)} = E$$

$$E - A = F$$

$$\frac{F}{E} \times 100 = G$$

Health Hazards

Listed below is a 'Kitchen, Fire, Health and Safety' checklist. Please follow these basic measures to ensure healthy food from your kitchen for you and your guests.

Practices:
1. Ensure dry goods are stored correctly and rotated
2. Date transfer labels in use on decanted dry products
3. Chilled food must be stored below 8°C
4. Chilled food must be day dotted correctly as per shelf life policy
5. Chilled food must be covered and rotated
6. Frozen food must be stored below -18°C
7. Defrosting food – must be day dotted as per shelf life policy and not stored at amebient
8. Cross contamination – use correct boards as stated on the next page and ensure knives are washed after use, don't take from one board to another. Also check storage of food (cooked food must be above raw meat, fish must always be kept below raw meat and eggs must be kept at the bottom of the fridge)
9. Spit roasting – ensure core temperature is checked (+75°C) with a probe and that it is working correctly. Alto Shaam temperature must be above +70°C
10. All hot hold food must be above +63°C

Cleaning:
1. Ensure a cleaning rota is in evidence and in use (check equipment on yesterdays rota)
2. Cleaning products available should be:
    a. D1 (washing up liquid) and D"2 (heavy duty cleaner)
    b. D10 (sanitiser) and DiverSol SW Tablets (Salad sanitising tablets)
3. Chemicals not attached should be locked in a chemical store
4. Ensure there is no evidence of grease

Food Boards:

It is suggested that you have 6 food preparation boards and that they each have a singular use. These boards are as follows:

Raw Meat – Red Board

Cooked Meat – Yellow board

Raw Fish – Blue Board

Fruit & Salad – Green Board

Vegetables – Orange board

Dairy Produce–White Board

Index

A

B

C

G

H

I

K

L

231